No Good

John Hope

No Good

Front and Back Cover images by Dorothea Lange
Licensing through Shorpy, Inc.

For more information regarding permissions,
Contact John Hope at: www.johnhopewriting.com

Summary: Twelve-year-old Johnny "No Good" and his newly adopted
brother Josh find themselves in the middle of a manhunt for a murderer
in 1940s Sanford, Florida when No Good discovers Josh is connected
with the prime suspect.

Flesch-Kincaid Reading Ease Score	**89.3**
Flesch-Kincaid Reading Level	**3.4 Grade**
Gunning-Fog Score	**5.5 Grade**
Coleman-Liau Index	**6.6 Grade**
SMOG Index	**3.9 Grade**
Recommended Reading Levels	**6-8 Grades,** **4-5 Grades Advanced**
Page Count	**136 pages**
Genre	**Historical Middle Grade**
Setting	**1947 Sanford, Florida**
Theme	**Acceptance, Racial & Family**

For teaching material and resources:
www.johnhopewriting.com

DEDICATION

To Jaime

One

One-Week Brother

When you're twelve and unwanted, big news like getting a new brother doesn't always make it to your ears. I sat at the kitchen table that evening rubbing my smooth, tired face, still a week away from being scarred for life. But I didn't know about the scar or my brother.

I watched Momma slice up celery and toss chunks into a giant boiling pot of stew. Her short, thin body was all hunched and tense like it always was, no matter what sort of mood she was in. Dusk was settling in and the mosquitoes were out, which meant Pa was on his way home from work.

"You eatin' with us, No Good?" Momma asked with her back toward me. Everyone I knew called me Johnny No Good, or just No Good—even my own parents. I don't remember how it got started, but by twelve it was so regular it didn't mean anything.

"Uh...naw." I always tried to fake a bit of indecision, as if I were giving up something I desired.

1

But then Momma gave her typical "Um," which always led me to think she knew I currently had a half-dozen oranges warming my gut.

"You heard from Uncle Travis yet?" I asked. It was 1947, two years after the end of the second world war. Yet Uncle Travis was still workin' for the army. He wasn't killing no one now days, but he still had a gun and I got excited every time he came home.

"I dun told you I'd let you know once I know when he'll be comin' in. Stop badgerin' me."

"He stationed in China?"

"Tokyo's in Japan, No Good. Don't they teach you nothin' in school? I swear, sometimes—"

The kitchen door flew open and I sat up in my chair expecting Pa. But it was just Tommy J. I sat back disappointed.

Tommy J came bouncing in shirtless, as he always was, with his typical I-know-something-you-don't smile. "Hey, Momma!"

"Hello, Tommy J," Momma answered, still not looking up from her celery.

Momma wasn't really Tommy J's momma. In fact, he didn't have parent one. I never knew what happened to his folks. I asked him a couple times, and he always said, "They on a trip!"; but I never saw them once the whole time I knew him. So Tommy J was sort of the neighborhood son. He'd stop in, eat dinner, maybe stay the night, and then scoot off the next morning to someone else's house. The only good part about Tommy J was how he always heard what was going on around town before anybody else. He'd known Mary Thompson was two-timing Old Man Nate with Cecil Jacobs long before she ever admitted it. He knew Pastor Dave was pinchin' from the till long before the old ladies from the 3-M club called him on it. Heck, he even knew about V-E day and V-J day about a week before either of them happened. The boy was a walking, talking tabloid.

2

Tommy J plopped down at the kitchen table opposite me and continued eating away at the apple in his sticky hands. He was twelve like me, but about hundred times dirtier—another thing I never understood about him. He didn't like sports and he was never out in the mud and dirt like most other kids, yet he was forever dirty as sin.

Momma stopped cutting and asked, "Any news, Tommy J?" Momma always had this rough look about her, but it got a touch softer when she was prying for something juicy. It was always the women who wanted the first word from Tommy J.

He took another bite from his apple and with a full mouth, he spat out, "Mr. Hank lost his job at White's."

"Ahhh…" She turned back to her celery. "I already heard that from Marge and Grace the other day."

"Yeah." He took another bite. "But I bet you ain't hear'ed how he got fired."

She stopped again and looked up at Tommy J.

"He was caught the night before doin' the deed down the produce aisle after hours."

Momma gasped. "No! Mr. Hank? With who?"

"None other than Li'l Miss Katy McGwire."

Momma let out a snort. "That little tramp." She shook her knife at Tommy J. "I been sayin' she 'uz up to no good for years. Don't think I forgot what she did at homecoming. And now she done got Mr. Hank fired. Na, uh. She got it comin', and I mean good." Momma turned back to the stew and gave it a few fast spins.

I looked at Tommy J. His face shone with the satisfaction that comes only when you know you've done a good job at what you do best.

I liked listening to Tommy J, but beyond his gossips, there was nothing to him. He never wanted to play, and he was always pinchin' off of other kids' spoils. Probably got some other kid to steal that apple he was eating. Besides, he always smelled like a dead animal. He never wore a shirt and was

3

forever red and sunburnt. And he was usually barefoot, though sometimes I'd catch him with a pair of the ugliest brown boots. I peeked under the table. No shoes.

I was so busy checking out Tommy J, it took me a minute to realize he was staring back at me. "Whatcha smilin' at, Tommy J?"

He sneaked a quick glance at Momma and then leaned forward and whispered, "I got news for you too, No Good."

I looked at Momma to see if she'd heard Tommy J. She just kept cutting and stirring. I frowned at Tommy J and whispered back, "Well, spill it."

He jerked his head toward the hallway. I followed him out the kitchen toward my bedroom. We went into my room and I closed the door. "Well?"

He smiled and took another bite of his apple. Tommy J was an artist at telling gossip. He knew coming right out with it was no way to go. You had to ease into it like slipping into a hot, steamy bath, slowly warming to the story.

"You ain't gonna like this," he said.

"Like what? Jist say it, will yeh?"

He smiled again and scraped another sliver of apple into his mouth with them crooked teeth of his. "Your Momma and Pa got a surprise for you tonight."

"A surprise?" I stood up straighter. "Well, what is it?"

"Your daddy ain't comin' straight home from work."

In my neighborhood, something like that usually meant your daddy was two-timin' with someone on the way home. But not my Pa. He wasn't no Sunday saint, but he wouldn't never do something like that to Momma.

"Whatcha mean he ain't comin' straight home?"

Tommy J smiled and scraped off another sliver of apple. "Well?"

"Someone in this room gonna have a new brother."

I took a step back and looked around. "Whatcha mean I'm getting a new brother? Whatcha heard, Tommy J?"

4

"Seems First Baptist been takin' in more orphans than it can handle lately. Seems your daddy and a few others been talkin' to Pastor Jim and made an offer to take a few of them off their hands 'til they find homes for them. Seems there's a kid about our age your daddy gonna pick up today on his way home." With his last words, Tommy J took a healthy bite of his apple and grimaced.

As I stood there silently, Tommy J spat seeds and apple core out onto my floor. I smacked that boy in the head. "Stop spittin' on my floor!" He was about to take another bite when I hit him again. "Pick that spit up!" I said.

He stuck the apple in his teeth and got down on his hands and knees to clean up the mess on the floor.

I stared at him, trying to make sense out of his gossip. I scratched my head. "You...well, how come Momma or Pa ain't said nothin'?"

He shrugged and continued to clean up the floor. Mumbling with the apple still in his teeth, "How shoo I oh, Oh Good?"

"You know everything else, Tommy J."

I marched to the kitchen. I stood there staring at the back of Momma's head, not knowing how to ask her about Tommy J's news.

Before I said a word, Momma spun around and looked me square in the eyes. "Tommy J tell you where Pa is?"

I dropped my jaw. "He... I... Well, how come you ain't said nothin' to me?"

She wiped her hands on a dishtowel. "No Good, we ain't even known 'bout this ourselves 'til three days ago."

"Three days? You knew 'bout this for three days?"

"No Good..." She tilted her head to the side. "Even we didn't know it was gonna happen for sure 'til today. Besides, we didn't want to have our hopes up. You know..."

Actually, I did know. About six months after I was born, right after droppin' me off at my nana's for the night, Momma

5

and Pa ran their car up into a tree in the middle of a tropical storm. They were with my Uncle Jacob and Aunt Jean, two folks I only ever knew from a photograph that hung in the living room. Well, Uncle Jacob and Aunt Jean died, Pa ended up with a permanent limp, and Momma hurt her insides right good and doctors said she was never gonna have kids again. Pa never took never for an answer, so he and Momma had been trying for another kid ever since.

I looked at Momma. She stared back at me with her dark frazzled hair, wearing that limp blue–and–white dress she used to wear to church. I wanted to say something, but there was nothin' to say to that. I'd had a little brother coming ever since I was six months old and there was nothin' I could do about it. And now, I was but a few minutes away from meeting him.

I turned and walked back to my room, passing Tommy J in the hall as I went. I wasn't mad anymore, but I wasn't altogether happy either. I closed the door, sat on my bed, and waited. I'd always thought I was going to have a little brother. I'd dreamt about it, even—maybe a hundred times. But I never really considered how I felt about it. On the one hand, I didn't need no brother hanging around. But on the other, maybe it wouldn't be too bad after all. Tommy J said he was our age. That meant no changing diapers or midnight feedings or any other crud my neighbors with babies did. He was just some kid. Some kid who I could tell what's what and set him straight so he didn't become another Tommy J—shirtless, shoeless, and pinching off everyone else.

I heard the rattle of the screen door and the muffled murmurs of Momma greeting someone. I couldn't hear her too well, but she was all kinds of talkative, and if I didn't know better, she sounded kind of like she was talking to an infant. I tried to listen closer. I could hear the rumble of Pa's voice, but I couldn't hear no kid talking. This got me worried. Did Pa bring home a baby instead?

6

I sat up in bed feeling even worse than before. Tommy J was occasionally wrong. Once he said Jeannie down the road had yellow fever and was sure to be a goner in a week, but then I caught her making out with some boy in the park just two days later.

I stood up and shot out my door toward the kitchen. I stopped at the end of the hallway and peeked around the corner.

Momma was blabbering on, "…but that ain't real food. They never give those kids at First Baptist enough. Sit yourself down and I'll…No Good!"

I jumped back out of sight.

"Now, No Good, get your butt out here and meet your new brother. Quit hidin' like you're afraid of him."

"I ain't afraid of nobody." I marched into plain sight.

And there he was, sitting at the end of the table where Pa usually sat. Pa was standing behind him with his hands resting on the kid's shoulders. Pa was a big man. Thin, but tall and stronger than a horse. He hovered over the boy like a giant osprey with a tiny mouse in its claws.

"Meet Josh, sport," Pa told me.

Josh didn't say anything. He just sat there looking partly scared, partly sad.

The first words out my mouth were: "He ain't no twelve-year-old. Tommy J said he was my age. Shoot, he can't be more than ten."

"Watch your tone, No Good," Momma snapped.

"Tommy J was right," said Pa. "Josh is twelve, just like you, sport."

Tommy J was standing along the wall next to Pa, smiling and no doubt taking mental notes. I just knew he'd be gossiping about me to every house up and down Celery Avenue. But I didn't care what Tommy J said.

I frowned and looked down at Josh. "He's a runt. No wonder no one else would take him."

7

Not a second later, Momma's spoon came slicing through the air and smacked me in the back of my thigh. I jumped and grabbed my leg.

"Ah! Dang nabbit!"

"Watch your mouth." She slapped me again with the spoon.

"Ah!" I jumped away.

Momma didn't hesitate. She reached out, grabbed my ear, gave it a twist, and dragged me down the hallway to my bedroom.

There, she let go of my ear and I fell back on my bed.

"Now, you listen here." Momma pointed the spoon at me. "Josh is here and here to stay, at least until... Well, he's here for a while. Whether you like it or not. Now you better learn how to speak to him like a decent human being or Pa won't be the only one who walks with a limp. You hearin' me?'

"Yeah, Momma. I'm hearin' you."

"Josh is family now. Our family. Now you stay in here until you can start treating Josh like he's your brother. 'Cause from now on, that's just what he is: your brother."

Momma spun around, marched out the door, and slammed it shut. I could hear her footsteps down the hallway. Her murmuring started up again and I could hear Pa's deep voice.

I eventually stopped trying to listen in and walked over to my bedroom window. The evening sky was dark and purplish. The light in my room was brighter than outdoors, so most of the outside world was hidden by the reflection of the junk in my room. Though invisible to me, I could hear the occasional tapping of moths hitting the window.

"My brother," I whispered. Nothing about this seemed real. Tommy J's gossip was always something going on out there. Nothing ever happened to us. We were boring, and I liked it that way. "My brother," I repeated, a little louder but still in a whisper. "Well...we'll see 'bout that."

Two

Clean' Up

I was still in my room, sitting on my bed and reading a book, when Josh came in. Momma shadowed him. I looked straight at him and he back at me—a little less glassy-eyed than at the table, but still as runt-like as ever.

Momma put her hands on Josh's shoulders. "Now, No Good. You treat him right or there's a wooden spoon with your name written all over it. Ya hear?"

I stared at Momma.

"I said, 'Ya hear?'"

"Yes, Momma."

"Now. Pa's fixin' to make him a bed, but that ain't gonna happen overnight so you two gonna have to share that bed of yours."

"Share my bed?"

"Don't you give me no lip, boy. That's the way it has to be." She patted Josh's shoulders and gave him a soft push forward. "You get yourself ready, Josh. I got the water on the stove now."

This was code for bathtime. I knew it well.

"We taking a bath?" I asked. "Tonight?"

Momma put both her hands on her hips and dropped her brow at me. "Now I jist done told you not to be flappin' your lip at me, No Good. Josh ain't had a decent washin' at First Baptist. Besides, you got so much filth behind them ears of yours, they 'bout set to grow a garden."

"But…" My mind searched for a way out. "Ain't we too old for you scrubbin' us down? Cully's been bathing himself since he was—"

"Now we've been through this before, No Good. You don't do that dirt justice. If you gonna be using up our hot water, it's gotta be done proper. I ain't gonna say this more than once. Git yourselves ready for a bath. Josh is first."

"Josh goin' first?" This was another blow. I always took a bath first. Now I had to sit in water with Josh's dirt and stink floating around me.

Momma gave me a stare that would've spoiled milk.

"Okay, Momma," I said quickly. "We gettin' ready."

Momma nodded slowly. She was set to leave when I spoke up.

"Momma?"

She turned back to me.

"Tommy J ain't still here, is he?"

Momma shook her head. "I shooed him off." She paused and then added, "And if you don't give me anymore of your lip, I'll consider fixin' you two some of them pancakes you like in the morning."

That got me all sorts of excited. "We havin' pancakes?"

"Now, this ain't gonna be a regular," Momma warned. "Jist a welcome to the family thing for Josh. We ain't made out of money, ya know."

She headed out and closed the door. And for the first time, I was alone with my new brother. Truth be told, I felt a bit uncomfortable around the kid. Don't know why. And to make things worse, I had to take off my clothes in front of him. I didn't even know the kid and he was gonna see me naked?

Josh seemed just as uneasy, standing there with his arms halfway folded together and looking around the room like it was some fancy art gallery.

"So," I said, which was about all I could think of at the time. Fortunately, my one-word greeting was enough to get him talking.

"You fixin' to get naked?"

This was the first time I heard him speak. His voice was about what I expected: higher-pitched then mine with a bit of gruff, like his throat was dry. His teeth surprised me. They were all dark and thin, like they hadn't ever met up with a toothbrush. They reminded me of Tommy J's.

"For the bath," Josh added.

"Well I ain't fixin' to git in there with my clothes on."

I inspected Josh's clothes. They were filthy and oversized, tattered around the edges. "You got your nightshirt?" He looked himself over and then up at me. "You get my bed all mucked up with them dirty clothes of yours and Momma's gonna whip us both raw."

"I…" Josh hesitated but then got out, "I ain't got no other clothes."

I was shocked. I had never even considered someone could be poorer than us. I at least had a coupla changes of clothes. "Ain't got no other clothes? Then watcha gonna sleep in?"

Without a word, Josh turned away, unbuttoned his overalls, yanked off his shirt, and let his overalls drop to the floor. Naked. He didn't even have underdrawers. He kicked off his clothes, curled his arms over his private parts, and turned to me.

I stepped from the bed, opened my dresser, and tossed Josh some underdrawers.

11

"You can sleep in these." Then I added, "But I don't wanna see no dookie stains in 'em."

Josh started to step into them.

"Watcha doin'? We still gonna bath. Just save them for bed."

Josh dropped my underdrawers next to his pile of clothes. With nothing on, Josh looked even skinnier, bones sticking out everywhere. He was as smooth as a baby. Wouldn't've surprise me if the kid hadn't been in fight one.

Josh's face had an expression that said, You next.

I answered him with, "I'll be there in a bit. You best git before Momma come and grab you by the ear."

He spun around and headed out to the kitchen where Momma was drawing up the bath. As he left, I saw some stripes down his back. He might never have been in a fight, but he'd no doubt gotten a few switch beatings.

From my bedroom, I heard Momma talking to Josh and him whispering something back to her. I plopped down on my bed in a huff. I was always the first in the tub before Momma and Pa. Not that I ever liked gettin' scrubbed raw with Momma's dishrags, but there was an understood privilege for gettin' in a clean tub without nobody else's filth swirling around me. Sitting alone in my room listening to the echoes of Josh getting scrubbed down, I felt as worthless as a bag of cow patties.

I stripped down to my underdrawers. I was going to kick them off too when I heard another splash from down the hall. I had walked naked through my house practically every Sunday morning before church to get my skin the dishrag treatment, but knowing Josh was there made me stop. I decided to keep my underdrawers on as I made my way to the kitchen.

As always, the kitchen table was pushed aside and the large round metal tub was center stage with Josh sitting in it like he wasn't but two years old.

Momma looked up from Josh. "What you got your underdrawers on for?"

"I'll kick them off when you're ready for me."

She returned her attention back to the kid in the tub. "Don't you be leaving your smelly skivvies in my kitchen."

I sat down on a chair and waited for my turn. I examined the tub. It was rusty and older than sin. My Grandma Emmerstaff used to scrub Pa in it when he was a kid. Inside it, Josh was swallowed up. He really had nothing of a body— narrow hips, sunken chest, and his arms and legs were thinner than a stickman.

"You sure are bony. We gotta get some meat on them bones."

"No Good!" Momma said, still intent on her scrubbing. "If you ain't got nothin' nice to say, you shut your pie hole."

"I'm just sayin' we could put some meat on them bones while he with us."

"Well, I ain't gonna be cookin' up a fortune just to fatten him up. We ain't made out of money, I tol' you."

I leaned in closer to look at the water. Dirt and various oils coagulated on the surface like moss on a blackwater creek. I grimaced at the thought of getting in after him. Then I noticed his gingerbread bobbing up and down, occasionally breaking the surface like a submerged turtle sipping air.

"No Good!" I jumped, immediately sitting back in the chair. Momma stopped scrubbing and glared at me. "What you doin' starin' at his gingerbread?"

I folded my arms. "I wusn't lookin' at nothin'."

She went back to scrubbing Josh. "Think you'd never seen one before."

"I wusn't lookin'," I repeated, practically pouting. I looked up at Josh. He turned away and smiled all bashful.

Leaning back, Momma wiped the sweat from her forehead. "Okay. Next up."

Josh stood up and stepped out of the tub. He grabbed the towel Momma held out for him and quickly wrapped it around himself. He stood there beside the tub staring back at me, as if waiting to catch a peek of my gingerbread. I held my hands on the rim of my underdrawers but couldn't bring myself to yank them down.

"I ain't waitin' all night, No Good," said Momma.

I looked at Momma, and then back at Josh. I tossed off the underdrawers and hopped into the tub. The tub's water splashed and got Momma good and wet.

"What you doin'?" She gave me a whack across the back of my head. "No Good, one day you gonna get it good. And I mean permanent."

I never quite understood most of Momma's threats, but I knew enough that she meant business. I sat there in the tub staring at Josh as he sat on the chair with the towel around his waist and stared right back at me. He took his time wiping himself down with the edges of the towel, but I caught him taking a peek or two into the tub. I tried to cover my gingerbread with my hands but Momma kept yanking my arms.

"No Good! Get them arms up. I need to get at them smelly pits of yours."

I still didn't know exactly what to think of this kid, but no doubt he was gonna be a pain in the butt.

"Josh," Momma said in the middle of a scrub. "I dun missed a whole patch of dirt on your front. No Good probably messed me up. Step back in the tub." Josh hesitated. "C'mon, step right in." I started to stand up, but Momma pushed me back down. "You stay, No Good. Don't wanna get splashed again. Besides, won't take but a second. C'mon, Josh."

Josh stood and stepped in, standing right in front of me with the towel still around his waist.

Momma grabbed Josh's towel. "No, don't get the towel wet," she said, tossing it aside.

14

Momma pulled him closer and started going at his belly with the dishrag. Meanwhile, I got a front row seat of Josh's gingerbread, dangling in front of my face and occasionally slapping my nose. I grimaced and turned away, squinting like I'd swallowed a stink bug. Josh struggled to keep himself from tipping over on top of me.

"There," Momma finally said letting go of Josh.

Josh, who was trying not to touch his gingerbread to my face, jerked back and lost his balance. He pinwheeled his arms, but his feet slipped on the tub's bottom he came crashing down into the water. It splashed up and got Momma even worse than when I got in.

"Ahhhh!" She fell back on her butt.

Sitting face-to-face in the tub, Josh and I looked at each other, and then we both burst out laughing like crazy.

"That wun't funny!" Momma yelled. "Now I'm soaked to the bone."

Josh and I kept right on laughin'.

Momma was steaming now. "Jist get outta here—both of yous! Before I smack you back to Tuesday."

Josh and I hopped out, grabbed our towels, and zipped off to my room before Momma could get her spoon. Josh tailed me all the way in and closed the door. We turned to each other and continued laughin'. But after a few seconds, I realized who I was laughin' with and I stopped. Josh stopped too, and we were left just staring at each other, both of us with our towels dangling in front of us.

We turned away from each other and threw on our underdrawers.

I stepped up to one side of my bed and he stepped up to the other. We stared at the bed like we were fixin' to climb into a coffin.

"Well…" I finally said, "if we goin' to bed, let's go to bed."

I clicked off my light and laid down. He laid next to me and I threw the sheets over us.

The longer I laid there, the more I could smell him. In spite of Momma's scrubbin', Josh still smelled like B.O. I thought about mentioning the stench, but I decided not to. After all, he wasn't all bad.

Three

Down the Stink Bug Trail

I awoke the next morning before Josh. I rolled out of bed, stood up, stretched, and then looked back at my bed. I put my foot up on the mattress and gave it a few bounces.

"Hey! Hey, get up!"

Josh's head bounced against the headboard and he sat up rubbing his hair.

"C'mon! I smell them pancakes cookin'."

We headed out of my room to the kitchen, and there was Momma cookin' away. We sat down and she served us up.

"Now don't you waste none," she told us.

I stuffed a pancake in my mouth. "Ain't no way!" I mumbled.

Momma smacked the back of my head, sending pancake bits flying. "Don't talk with your mouth full!"

After we'd completely stuffed ourselves, I lent Josh some clothes while Momma washed his, and I took him out to show him off to the neighborhood.

My neighborhood wasn't much to look at, but it was home. Each street was the same, lined on either side with dark rows of old Florida oaks. Each house had the same boxy wood frame design, all stained with oak sap and mold, and many covered with overgrown vines and weeds. Each had the same small porch in front, but differed in what kind of clutter was piled on it or who was sitting out front smoking or drinking.

I led Josh down to the street. We hopped over a row of short hedges that separated our property from that of Old Man Jones, who sat on his porch with some other old guy I didn't know. Both were smoking pipes as they rocked in squeaky chairs.

"Hey, Old Man Jones!" I waved.

"No Good." His voice crackled as he nodded. "Who's y'friend?"

"He ain't no friend." I stepped up to the porch and placed my arm around Josh's shoulders. "This here's my brother, Josh. Pa fetched him out of them First Baptist orphans."

Old Man Jones let out a long smoker's cough that seemed to last forever and then said, "Welcome to the neighborhood, Josh. Could've done better, though. Stuck with No Good."

"Na," I said. "I'll treat him good. I lent him my clothes already."

"That ain't nothin'. I meant he coulda been snatched up by one of them wealthy pilots that got so much money they use cash for a snot-rag. Coulda done real good with one a them folks, yes sir." He removed his pipe from his mouth and pointed it at me. "You keep outta trouble, ya hear? Both o' yous." He bit down onto the end of his pipe with a snarl.

The other old man spoke with a deep, throaty voice. "Why people have kids these days is beyond me. Don't see me with kids, no sir. Nothin' but trouble."

"We gotta get goin'," I said quickly. "Bye!" I darted off, dragging Josh with me. When we were out of earshot, I told him, "Don't worry 'bout them. They be dead soon, anyhow."

Just down the sidewalk, a gaunt middle-aged woman carried a huge pile of clothes in both arms. "That's Mrs. Johnston. She does the laundry for about half the city and gots to walk about twenty miles a day deliverin' it."

I pointed to a boy climbing a tree beside the next house we passed. "That's Ansel up there. He's about five years old and don't speak more than five or six words. Ain't never heard a full sentence out of him. Think somethin' not right in the boy's head."

Next I pointed to an old gray-haired lady watering her flowers outside her front door. "That's Miss Maples. She's a busybody, always up in everyone's business. Anytime somethin' going on, she all up into it."

I spotted a skinny girl standing on a porch across the street who was slappin' and yellin' at a pair of guys in army khakis. "Oh, yeah. That's Norma Rae right there. Keep away from her. She's stank. She got the clap a few years back and been spreadin' it around to every airdale she could get ever since. You know what the clap is?"

Josh shook his head.

"It's when you get all red and rashy down there," I pointed to my private parts. "And some fellas get it so bad, their gingerbread pops right off and they gotta spend the rest of their lives sittin' down to take a piss. Can you believe that?"

I spotted my friend Cully up the street. "Hey, Cully! Check out my new brother!" I pointed at Josh. "Cully!"

Cully acted like he couldn't hear me.

I turned back to Josh. "C'mon."

I started running across the street toward Cully's house, but stopped dead as a car slammed on its brakes and nearly ran me down. I fell into the hood and slid off and rolled onto the street.

When I looked up, the car's driver was staring me down through the open driver-side window. It was a cop. But worse than that, it was Officer Carter. The man was fatter than a

19

pregnant cow and he liked driving through our neighborhood about as much as eating a bag of rotten apples.

"No Good! Shoulda knew that was you. You ain't never lookin' where you goin'!" He hung his arm out his window, waggin' it like he was addressing a dog.

Josh stepped forward and gave me a hand. I grabbed it and stood up.

Officer Carter looked Josh over. "Now who we got here?"

"This my brother, Josh."

"Now I know your momma and daddy, No Good, and I know your momma's womb's all dried up. Besides he ain't no newborn, so why don't you knock off your storytellin'."

"I ain't storytellin'. He—"

"I ain't got time for this foolishness. Now, Jacob or Jerry or…"

"It's Josh," I said.

"I know the boy's name and you can see I'm talkin', so why don't you jist shut your big mouth? Now, Josh, I'm the law around here so if you know what's best, you keep your nose clean and we gonna get along jist fine. You understand what I'm sayin'?"

Josh nodded.

"Excuse me?"

"Yes."

"Yes? Now, I am an officer of the law. When you answer me, I expect a certain protocol. You tell me 'yes' and I'm gonna expect a 'sir' to follow. You know what I mean, boy?"

"Yes, sir."

"Alright, then." Officer Carter turned to me. "You keep out of trouble, No Good."

He drove off.

Josh and I stood there in the street, watching the cop car make its way down. I put a hand on Josh's shoulder and told him, "I know what you thinkin', so I'll go ahead and say it for you." I looked back toward the cop car and said, "That man's a cert-u-fied pain in the butt." I turned back to Josh and he was giving me a smile with those thin, black teeth of his. I smiled back. "C'mon. I'm sure Cully got some trouble for us to get into."

We took off to Cully's house.

Cully was my age and about my height, but was broader in his face and shoulders, the kind of kid you could tell would be fat in about ten years or so. He had curly dirty-blond hair that was always matted and wild no matter what state he was in, with a few curls dangling in his face.

When Josh and I stepped up the porch, Cully had that familiar wild look in his eyes, like something was about to happen. He paced the creaky wood planks that spanned the width of his house, like a soon-to-be daddy waiting for the kid to pop out.

"What's got you in a hissy?" I asked.

"Oh nothin', No Good. Jist waitin' for that nothin' of a sister—" His head jerked up and Josh and I followed his gaze down the street.

Jeannie, his sister, staggered down the sidewalk toward the house. She looked like she had just hopped off a merry-go-round after riding it five days straight.

Cully stuck his two little fingers in his mouth and let out a loud whistle. "Jeannie! Git your butt home, girl!"

Jeannie crossed Cully's front yard at an angle. "You ain't my daddy, you idget."

"I ain't gonna be hangin' 'round here babysittin' Grandpappy all day. I got—"

"Besides, you ain't but eleven, baby brother." Jeannie kept talking slur-mouthed like Cully hadn't said a word. "You ain't got nowhere to go."

"I'm twelve!"

Jeannie lumbered up the porch steps, pulling on the railing with both hands. "Besides, I'm but two years from gettin'

21

out of this dump anyhow. I don't need no curfew. Oh, hello." She brightened up at the sight of Josh and me.

"Hi, Jeannie," I said.

"And who's the cutie?" She flicked Josh's collar.

He stepped backwards, as if trying to avoid the embarrassment.

Cully came to the rescue with two fingers pushing her back. "Knock it off, will ya?"

"Don't be hasslin' me. And where's Grandpappy?"

"Got him listenin' to the radio. Later!" Cully jumped down the porch steps in one hop and looked back at Josh and me. "Well, ain't you comin'?"

Without a word, Josh and I whipped around Jeannie and raced down the street with Cully in the lead. I didn't know what Cully was up to or where he was heading, but I knew him enough to be sure it was going to be as fun as a twister in a trailer park.

After swinging around the corner out of sight of his house, we all slowed to a walk. Cully turned around to me. "So, who's the twig?"

"He ain't no twig! This my brother, Josh." I gave Josh a good smack across the shoulders, which about knocked him over.

Cully gave him a look-down. "You ain't got no brother."

"Do now. Pa picked him up from First Baptist. He one of them orphans."

Cully looked at Josh again. "What… D'you poop him out?"

I gave Cully a punch in the shoulder. "Take it back."

He shook his head. "He's skinnier than grass." Cully punched me back just to even things out. Then he turned his attention to Josh. "Hey, kid. Pick your shirt up. Go ahead, pick it up."

Josh looked over at me and then pulled the bottom of his shirt up to his chest.

22

Cully let out a laugh that sounded almost like a cough. "Shoot, boy. I almost see right through you."

Josh dropped his shirt. By this time, I was done with Cully's questions. "So where you headin' us off to, Cully?"

He gave me one of his half-cocked smiles and took off walkin' with a little giddy-up in his step.

"What?" I pressed. "C'mon, what?"

He glanced back. "I'm about to prove you wrong."

"Huh?" Then I realized what he meant. "You don't mean…"

"Yup. He's back. And I'm tellin' you, he's cookin' up a curse that'll have you drinkin' piss and crappin' out your ears by nightfall. And that's just for starters."

"A curse?" Josh spoke up.

"Ah, don't let Cully spook ya. He's just talkin' about Old Man Badeau. He's this old Negro who comes wanderin' into town on occasion."

"He ain't just an old Negro," said Cully. "He's half-Cajun and word is he got the devil in him."

"He from Goldsboro?" Josh asked.

"Goldsboro?" Cully snapped his head. "Don't you know nothin'? Goldsboro where all them educated Negros in suits come from. Old Man Badeau? No way. He the devil."

"That's just hogwash," I said.

"It ain't. You remember Mr. Peterson, down the way? He was drivin' down forty-four and picked up Old Man Badeau to give him a lift. Mr. Peterson ain't been heard from since. But sometimes at night you can hear a man callin' out 'Ruthie! Ruthie!' That's Mr. Peterson's old girl. And she died 'bout five years ago."

I shook my head and turned to Josh. "Don't believe that for a second. Pa said Mr. Peterson went up north for some schoolin' and he's comin' back any day now."

"And how long's any day now been?" countered Cully. "I'm tellin' ya, he's as dead as a rock. And cursed. Oh, yeah. He's cursed for sure. The devil got him good."

It was no use arguin' further. Cully was as stubborn as an old dog and refused to believe he was ever wrong. He'd argue the spelling of words with the teacher even with the dictionary sayin' otherwise.

We made our way through a marshy path that skirted the southeast edge of Lake Monroe. We all called this path the Stink Bug Trail, since you squished so many red bugs jumping from one squishy log to the next that you stank to high heaven by the time you got yourself out of there.

We had barely crossed over the first few mossy logs when Josh slipped on a mess of bugs and landed butt-first into a small pool of mud. Cully laughed so hard, he about cracked a rib.

"C'mon, Josh," I said, picking him up by his bony arm. "Watch where you goin'. You're gettin' my clothes all muddy." I took a swipe at the back of my pants he was wearing.

Josh tried to brush the rest of the mud off, but got his hands all mucked up. I watched him try to wipe them off on a bush, but he grabbed some thorny ivy, which nearly sliced his fingers right off. Josh stuck his hands in his armpits and winced.

I stopped. "Well, shoot boy. What'd you expect? Don't you know thorns when you see 'em?"

"Now what he done?" asked Cully.

"Ah. Never you mind."

Josh examined his hands; the cuts were turning reddish brown. I grabbed a frond from a shrubby palm and peeled it into strips and wrapped them around Josh's palms.

Cully was by now a few trees ahead of us. "Hey! C'mon, already," he called, then took off again.

"We comin'!" I turned to Josh. "Just do what I do, and don't do nuthin' else stupid."

We had to pick up our pace to catch up to Cully. Before I could bug him again about where he was leading us, he slowed up. He lowered his head and shoulders and walked all quiet-like, like he was sneaking through a place he don't belong. Josh and I followed, stooping and inching our way along. Cully got up behind a pair of bushes and laid belly-first on the ground. Josh and I stooped down on either side of him.

Through the bushes about twenty feet or so away, we could see the back of the head of a Negro man who was sitting on the other side of a fallen tree. Beyond him was Lake Monroe, quiet and motionless except for the occasional soundless circles made by mosquitoes jumping along the surface. The man had a streaky gray and black poof of hair around his head, making it appear twice the size it really was. He was jerking back and forth, but from our vantage point it was hard to tell why.

"That's him," whispered Cully. "Old Man Badeau."

"What's he doin'?" I whispered.

"Who knows? Fixin' to eat a live animal. Mixing up a potion. No tellin' what that wacky goon is up to."

Before I could venture a guess, Old Man Badeau stood up and stepped away from the log. His long, naked Negro body stared back at us, his sagging butt cheeks wobbling with each step. He continued on toward the lake and waded in up to his chest, then he lunged forward into the water. He went right into a swim, kicking and stroking his way through the water like a machine.

"Where's he goin'?" said Cully. He sat up and pushed his way through the bushes for a better view.

Josh and I came out of the bushes next to him and watched the old Negro swim away. About three-quarters of a mile ahead of him was a hunk of land that jutted out into the giant lake. It was dense with bushes and scrubby palms and looked like a bunch of nothin'.

"Think he's headin' out toward that?" I asked, pointing.

25

"He's a good swimmer," said Josh.

"I didn't know Negros could swim," I replied.

"They can't," said Cully. "But Old Man Badeau…I tell you what, that man's got the power of the devil, fer sure."

"That ain't so," said Josh.

"Oh really, skinny boy? What do you know about Negros anyhow?" Cully paused. "C'mon." He hopped on over the log Old Man Badeau had been sitting against.

Josh and I climbed up the log and saw Cully digging through Old Man Badeau's clothes.

"What you doin'?" I said.

The clothes looked like a bunch of rags piled up on a pair of tattered boots a couple sizes bigger than Pa's shoes.

Cully grabbed one of the boots and lifted it up to his head. "Would you look at the size of this? Hot damn."

I squatted down and grimaced. "Pee-yoo. Them things smell like a dead armadillo."

"Look!" called out Josh.

Cully and I swiveled our heads where Josh was pointing, out over the lake. Old Man Badeau wasn't swimmin' no more, just treadin' water and staring right back at us. Then he started up again, but this time swimming straight toward us.

I leapt off the log and was about to bolt when Cully called out to me and Josh. "Hey! Help me with this."

I turned and saw Cully gathering up Old Man Badeau's clothes in his arms.

"You crazy? What we need his clothes for?"

Josh darted back toward Cully and picked up a boot and handkerchief. Already holding the rest of his clothes, Cully said, "C'mon! Git on out."

We hightailed it out of there. Every step of the way, I could feel Old Man Badeau bearing down on us. We had a least half a minute on the man, but I had no idea how fast he could run. I kept a step behind Josh, 'cause I just knew he was going to slip on one of the logs we were jumping over. Sure enough,

26

we hit one covered in red bugs, and Josh slid right off. I picked up the boot and handkerchief he'd been carrying and yelled "Git up!" as I pushed the boy back up onto his feet. We took off runnin' through the Stink Bug Trail, zippin' around logs and bushes like rabbits on fire.

When we finally came out of the trail, we kept right on running, down one street then another. I rounded a corner and tripped over Josh who had stopped all of a sudden. Josh and I hit the ground hard and rolled. Bouncing back up, I picked up the boot but couldn't find the handkerchief. I looked up, and Cully was already a half-block away. I patted Josh's back as he got to his feet, and we took off toward Cully.

Cully rounded another corner and immediately halted. Josh and I practically slammed into the back of him before we realized the reason. About ten feet in front of us was Officer Carter, standing next to his squad car staring straight back at us.

He lifted his chubby hands to his hips and spoke all slow-like. "I'm almost too afraid to ask, but what've you three gotten yourselves into? I should've known better than to trust you, No Good."

Cully spoke up. "We ain't doin' nothin'."

"Excuse me? 'We ain't doin' nothin'?" Officer Carter swaggered up to us. "Boy, that ain't no way to speak to an officer of the law. Now I better start hearin' some proper protocol or I'll be kickin' your little butts into jail faster than a mule with an attitude."

We all spoke at once. "Yeah, yes. Yes, sir. Sir, yes, sir."

Officer Carter, now towering in front of us with his big ol' belly, ordered, "Now you gonna tell me whose clothes those are, or do I have to tell your mommas it's past time to redden your little backsides again?"

"They ain't nobody's," I told him. "...Uh, sir."

"'Ain't nobody's'?" He snatched the boot from my hands. "Nobody got a bare foot lookin' for this? What the...? This smells like a dead armadillo."

"We found it," Cully told him. "We don't know whose it be."

"Well if it ain't nobody's," said Officer Carter, "then why you runnin'?" He looked at the boot again. "Besides, anything that smelly…someone worn it not too long ago. Probably searchin' for it right now."

I thought about Old Man Badeau, who was no doubt running naked through the woods hunting us down. I didn't dare turn around to check for him, though. That'd incriminate us for sure. Fortunately, Josh and Cully didn't look neither.

Officer Carter continued. "And why the tarnation does…Jared…"

"Josh," I offered up.

"Josh!" Officer Carter spat the name out as if he wanted to say it first. "Why the tarnation does Josh have palm fronds wrapped around his hands?"

I stuttered, "Uh…it's…them for boxing."

"Boxing?" the large man repeated.

"Yeah," Cully joined in. "Show him your boxing moves, Josh."

Awkwardly, Josh made a few air punches toward me, until the big man said, "All right, all right."

Officer Carter stared us down for a few long seconds and then said, "I do hate kids. Whether you lyin' or honest, someone'll be lookin' for these clothes in no time. Hand them over. I mean now!" Cully handed him the pile of clothes and the other boot. "Next time you happen upon somethin' that ain't yours, don't you be hightailin' it off like the Collins' ghost chasin' you down. Now, get on home before you find yourselves in real trouble. Git!"

Prizeless, Cully, Josh, and I took off runnin' toward Cully's house. We got to Cully's front porch and stopped to catch our breaths.

"What made you take that man's clothes anyhow?" I asked Cully. "We were that close to getting our butts whupped somethin' fierce."

"Ah…" Cully shrugged. This was often his response to brainless acts of nonsense he somehow wrangled me into.

*   *   *

That evening, Momma, Pa, Josh, and I were sitting around the kitchen table eating when Josh reached for a bowl of biscuits. Momma snatched his arm and rotated it, exposing the scratches running down his palm. The lines were already darkened. "What'd you do with Josh's hand, No Good?"

I replied with my mouth stuffed with vegetables. "I ain't done nothin'."

"I'd be a king's fool to believe you ain't the cause of this."

Josh spoke weakly as he slid his hand out of Momma's grip. "It don't hurt none."

"Don't let No Good brainwash ya. If he's beaten up on you—"

"Emily, please," Pa spoke up. "It's just a few scratches. Boys will be boys. Probably grabbed a few thorns by mistake."

"'Boys will be boys,'" Momma scoffed. "Just my luck to be surrounded by boys. Momma always told me havin' boys be nothin' but trouble. In my next life, it'll be all girls for me, that's for sure. And I don't mean no tomboys, neither. All lady to the T." She grabbed herself a biscuit and bit into it like she was biting the head off an animal.

*   *   *

That night, Josh and I were gettin' set for bed when Josh closed my bedroom door.

"It don't got to be closed," I told him. "Besides, it gets hot some—" I stopped, seeing the peculiar grin on Josh's face. "Now what you cookin' up?"

Out of the blue, Josh stuck his hand straight down into his pants.

"What the…" But before I could finish my thought, he fished around and yanked out the ugliest, dirtiest handkerchief I'd ever seen. "Is that…?"

Josh nodded.

"Can I hold it?" I took it from Josh and rolled it around my hands. I stared at it as if it were an ancient Egyptian relic. It smelled musty and felt slightly damp. As I handed it back to Josh, it occurred to me that the smelly handkerchief had been tucked against Josh's gingerbread ever since this morning's romp down the Stink Bug Trail. I sniffed my hands and sure enough, they smelled of piss.

Josh held the handkerchief and studied my face. "You think it's cursed, don't cha?"

I shook my head and rubbed my hands against my shirt to wipe off the smell. "Na. That's all hogwash. But all the same, I wouldn't be hangin' on to that thing. That old Negro so nuts in the head, never know what he'd do if he catch you with it."

"I wanna give it back."

"Go back to Old Man Badeau? You crazy? You think he'd just take it back like it's nothing? Boy, you dumber than I thought. It might have been Cully's dumb idea to take it, but now that's taken, you can't give it back."

"Why you think they call him Old Man Badeau?"

I frowned at him. "Now, what else you think we should call 'im?"

Josh looked away. "Don't know. It's jist…I don't think he look like an Old Man Badeau."

"Now, how could you tell? We barely see'd him from the back."

30

"It's jist…a name hasta fit the man. Old Man Badeau jist don't seem to fit him none."

I frowned at the boy again. I didn't know where he was comin' up with this stuff. A name fitting a man and all that. He was just talking crazy.

"C'mon," I said, waving him to bed.

We shut off the light and laid down. As I lay there, I could feel Josh moving around and I could smell that nasty handkerchief. I tried to ignore it, but it was so rank I couldn't help rubbing my nose every few seconds trying to wipe out the scent.

"Would ya throw that thing out on the porch or somethin'? It stinks somethin' awful."

Josh got out of bed and left the room. I thought about Josh and that nasty handkerchief. As terrible as it was that Josh took it from that old Negro, he was just doin' what Cully told him to do. If I were a new brother not knowin' any better, I'd probably do the same. Plus, of us three, he was the only one who slipped it past Officer Carter. He didn't even let on to Cully he had it. Just kept it tucked in his drawers all day waitin' for nightfall before he whipped it out. Gotta give a guy respect for figurin' out who to trust in just a day's time.

A minute later, he came back in, felt his way around, and climbed back in bed. After he got settled in, I said, "Hey, Josh."

"Yeah?"

"You…you all right."

He didn't say nothin' back.

We laid there listening to the crickets outside and the creaks of the house and Momma and Pa's footsteps out in the hallway. I closed my eyes.

Four

Cully

The next morning I woke alone. It took me several seconds to figure out that waking up alone was not right. I sat up and searched around.

Straining, I called out, "Josh?" And then I coughed out some of the night from my throat. I got up and searched around the house. No Josh. I headed outside and took my morning piss next to the oak tree behind the house; still no Josh.

I headed inside and sat down at the kitchen table. Momma came bustling in like she'd been awake for the past couple hours. She glanced my way as she poured herself another cup of coffee.

"Where's Josh?" she asked.

He'd only been my brother for about a day and a half, but that whole time he hadn't been more than ten feet from my side. I looked up at Momma, not knowing how to answer her. I felt a chill on my face.

I took a breath and was about to admit that I had lost him, when Josh came strolling into the kitchen from the hallway.

"Mornin', Josh," Momma said. "You lookin' chipper."

Josh sat down at the table and smiled at me.

"Yeah," he said.

Josh had a few beads of sweat dripping out from the tips of his floppy hair, and he was breathing too heavy for just waking up.

"You gettin' use to sharin' a bed with No Good?" Momma asked. "Or did you share beds at First Baptist?"

"We had cots," he said. Then added, "Army cots."

"Imagine that." Momma sat down at the table holding her coffee cup in both hands. "Ever wonder who had them cots? Coulda been some ace fighter pilot or some army hero." Momma always got all sorts of excited seeing men in uniform. Unlike most wives, she actually wanted Pa to sign up during the war, but his bad eyes and flat feet kept him out. One time Pa signed up to be the volunteer officer in charge of all that metal and animal fat they were collecting, and he came home once a week in uniform. And once a week like clockwork, I'd hear 'em through the walls, workin' on getting me a little brother.

"I guess," Josh said.

"Josh," I said. "How come you don't say more than three words at a time? Can't you ever say a full sentence?"

"No Good!" Momma snapped. "Don't you ever got nothing nice to say? He ain't been here more than two days and you been ripping into him ever since. Now, you apologize right now, and while you at it, say something nice to him."

"Somethin' nice?"

"Or can't you manage a full sentence?"

I turned to Josh. "Sorry," I said. "And...uh, you got nice eyes."

Josh giggled and looked away.

"No Good, you hopeless."

33

"What? You told me say somethin' nice. What'd you want me to say?"

She shook her head. "You just gotta be a gentlemen, that's all. You ain't gotta kiss his butt. How 'bout, 'Good morning, Josh' or 'You lookin' chipper today, Josh.' Just make him feel like one of the family, that's all."

"One of the family? So I should call him 'No Good'?"

Momma went to speak but then stopped. She stared at me hard and then said in one of the softest tones I'd ever heard from her, "No, Johnny."

I hadn't heard Momma utter the name Johnny since I was about five. It was so foreign coming from her, it almost didn't even sound like my name. Momma gave me a look that didn't make me feel right. I turned away.

Momma didn't say no more, and although I was facing away from her, I felt her stare.

Wanting to leave, I said to Josh, "C'mon. Cully and I got a job for you." I stood up and turned to Momma. "It ain't nothin' bad."

She was smiling at me. "Go on." But when Josh stood up, Momma said, "Wait. You two ain't eatin'?"

Josh looked like he was about to sit back down when I spoke up. "No. We'll manage. C'mon, Josh."

Cautiously, Josh followed me as I scooted out the back door.

Josh ran like a puppy trying to keep up. "Where we goin'?" But I could hear by the way he asked it that what he meant was: "How come we didn't stay for breakfast?"

I knew a kid as skinny as Josh probably had skipped a few more meals than he ever wanted to. But it was Saturday mornin', and me and my friends had a tradition I knew Josh would like. "Don't you worry 'bout that. Just as long as you keep up."

We headed down a few streets until we came to the far end of Reed's groves. Mr. Reed had a few acres of orange groves. The trees were planted in perfect lines, and each row was so thick, it was a perfect place to play tag. Hidin' places would come and go as you ran from row to row, making you feel dizzy. But best of all, after you were done, you could help yourself to a heap of oranges.

I jumped into a dried ditch next to the white picket fence surrounding the groves. Josh wiggled up next to me like a snake, and both of us took in the greens and the sweet scent of orange blossoms wafting at us. I closed my eyes and breathed it in.

"Now what?" Josh asked.

"Hold your horses."

A minute later, we heard the panting of a few kids coming from behind. We turned around just in time to see Cully and Jacob and Seth hopping down into the ditch.

Jacob and Seth were brothers who looked nothing alike. But they practically shared a brain. It seemed at times like whatever one was thinking, the other would come right out and say. They were both poor-thin, but neither as scrawny as Josh. And they were as ugly as sick goats. Seth had dark curly hair and a bum ear since birth that was twisted and small. Jacob was taller and older with wild dirty-blond hair that looked like it hadn't been washed for about ten years. Jacob had broken his leg a few years back, and since his daddy couldn't afford a doctor worth a wooden nickel, the leg never set right and he'd walked with a limp ever since. And when he ran, he skipped along every other step like a pirate with a peg leg.

"What took you so long?" I asked the threesome. "We been here forever waitin' for y'all."

"I was waitin' for these two slow clodhoppers," said Cully. "Had to drag them out of bed."

Jacob sized up Josh. "He that orphan?"

"His name's Josh," I said. "He ain't an orphan no more. He's m'brother."

"He may be your brother now," Jacob shot back, "but he'll always be an orphan. Ya can't stop being an orphan."

35

"Says who?"

Seth interrupted. "We gonna eat, or flap our jaws all mornin'?" He always spoke with a screechy strain, as if that bum ear of his stretched out his voice.

Before anyone could answer, a rumbling sound came echoing from above. We searched the sky, looking this way and that, until a pair of giant Navy planes with four engines on each of their wings popped out of a cloud and flew right above our heads. It wasn't look uncommon to see these flying this way or that, but they always pulled our attention away and we stared at them like they were aliens coming to visit. We remained quiet until they passed.

"We gonna play tag or what?" asked Jacob.

"I'd eat my good ear, I'm so hungry." said Seth.

"Shoot, boy," I said. "Guess we'll eat before Seth gets all cannibal."

Cully started our game. "Well…seems them Japs stole our hand grenades. Looks like we gotta steal them back."

"Ah, hand grenades?" Jacob complained.

Cully turned to Jacob. "You can think of somethin' better?"

"Na," said Seth. "Let's get goin'."

"Okay, on three," said Cully. "One, two, three…charge!"

Cully, Jacob, Seth, and I charged over the edge of the ditch and vaulted over the fence. Hitting the ground on the other side, I checked over my shoulder for Josh and saw him struggling to get over.

"C'mon, Josh!" I jumped in place.

When he finally made it, I waved him to follow me and took off running down a row of groves. Passing tree after tree, I kept my eyes peeled for a ripe orange.

Still running, I turned back to Josh and said, "Let's try over there."

We cut through a tight gap between a pair of groves and cut through the next couple gaps. After squeezing through the fourth gap, we came upon a row of trees that were bigger than in the previous rows. I turned down the row and scanned for hanging fruit. I slowed. My eyes passed by dozens of little green buds. Then, like a shining light, a pair of bright oranges hung out on one of the limbs.

"There!" I pointed and made a beeline to the fruit.

Sliding along the dirt on my folded legs, I reached out and plucked off the first ripe orange. Reaching over to the next branch, I plucked off the second one. I felt Josh's body smack into the back of mine. I spun around and tossed him one of the fruits. He caught it and looked it over like he ain't never seen an orange before.

"Just hold on to it," I told him. "Let's get some more over—"

SLAM! The sound of a door echoed out in the distance. I spun my head around. I couldn't see anyone, but I could hear a man yelling curses from behind me. He sounded close and mad.

"C'mon," I said. "The Japs are comin'."

Sliding out from underneath the grove, I jumped to my feet and ran for my life. I stole a glance behind me. Josh was running as fast as he could, barely keeping up. I turned forward again and slammed face-first into a wall. I bounced back and landed square on my butt. After rubbing the stars out of my face, I looked up to see that the wall was a giant of a man wearing overalls and a John Deere hat. He stared at me like a gorilla right after I stole his banana.

"Whatcha doin' here, boy?" his deep voice thundered. "Ain't no place for chilluns." The man was white, but he was so dirty he looked like a Negro.

I looked behind me and saw nothing but empty rows of trees. Josh was nowhere. I turned back to the giant. "We was playin' tag and I got lost."

"Tag? You'll be playin' tag all the way to the jailhouse if I catch you here again. Now, git!" He thumbed his giant hand to the side.

I stumbled to my feet and tried to run, when the man's huge hand stopped me.

"Hold on. Whatcha got in your hand, boy?"

I looked down. I was holding the orange. I looked back up. "Found it on the ground."

He furrowed his brow. "Bull…"

Quivering there under the giant's shadow, I wondered how I was going to get myself out of this. And then it got worse. A second giant emerged from behind the first one. This one was even bigger; overalls, bulging muscles, and a stench that'd stall a car.

"What's this?"

"Thief," the first one replied, pointing to the orange still in my hand.

"Thief?" The second took a step toward me. He spoke with a pulverizing nicotine grumble, like he was grinding his teeth into sand. "Mmmmm…I hate thieves!"

I swallowed and took a small step back. Each of them took a massive step toward me. My heart bounced around inside me so hard, it was about to pop. I could feel my stomach inching up my throat. I opened my mouth to speak. "I—"

An orange came hurtling out from the sky and smacked me like a rock across my face. I stumbled back a step, and I could feel my upper cheek swell.

I shook away the sting and looked up to see the giants spinning around, confused. Seeing my chance, I bolted, my legs pumping like crazy. I could hear the sound of the giants yelling from behind, but I didn't waste a millisecond to look back.

I cut through row after row of groves, zigzagging closer and closer to the edge of the property. I wheeled around the last grove and almost ran smack into the white picket fence. I vaulted over.

Hitting the ground on the other side, I kept right on running; past the surrounding ditch, down Reed Street, and around the corner and the next corner and the next. I didn't stop running until I reached my street, and even then I slowed up only a pinch to catch my breath.

It was then I remembered Josh. I slowedup more and looked back. There was no one behind me as far as I could see. Cully, Jacob, Seth, and I have all had our share of running away from angry farm hands in the past, so I wasn't worried about them. Just Josh.

I bit my lip and I headed back to Reed's groves. Hopping back into the ditch, I peeked over the embankment and through the white fence.

Everything seemed quiet. I didn't see nobody, kid or adult. I didn't like it. I knew one thing for sure: When a guy's sneaking around and can't find what he's looking for, something else is bound to find him.

Scanning quickly around, I ran away again. This time, I headed over to a patch of woods where Cully liked to hide out and smoke a couple of his grandpappy's cigarettes. Leaving the street, I cut through a thick section of bushes, hopped over a few familiar logs, and crossed a set of railroad tracks. Before I rounded the stack of logs that separated the tracks from Cully's hiding spot, I could hear Jacob and Seth laughin' like nobody's business.

"There he is!" Cully announced.

My feet slapped the leafy ground and I tried to catch my breath. I looked over the faces of my friends—and Josh. They were all relaxing, not one of them out of breath like me. Josh was the only one not smiling, but his eyes lit up as soon as he saw me. Cully had a cigarette between a couple fingers and was hunched over a stack of railroad ties like an old man on a smoke break.

"Where you been?" asked Seth. "Even Jacob beat you with his bum leg."

"Yeah," said Jacob. "Thought them hands had you, fer sure."

"Ain't no way," I said, still breathing hard. "Them fat lards can't catch me. I just—"

"How's your face?" Cully broke in and laughed.

I rubbed the side of my face where the orange had hit and frowned at Cully. "That was you? Why you smackin' me with an orange?"

Cully laughed again.

"You aim so bad you couldn't take out them hands?" I added.

"I didn't hit you with no orange." Cully took a drag of his grandpappy's cigarette. "That was Josh."

"Josh?" I spun around to my new brother. He looked away and then up at me shyly. "Wha…Josh?" I said, rubbing my head.

"Only had one orange," he said.

"So?"

"There're two of them. One of you."

"Yeah," Jacob said. "So he smacked you. Smacked you good! Me and Seth saw it."

I opened my mouth to say something else, but then I saw the genius. When Josh hit me, it distracted them farm hands just enough to let me get out of there. If he'da just hit one of the hands, it probably woulda just bounced off their rock-hard bodies and not made a spit of difference to either one. An orange hitting me, that was just strange enough to make them both wonder, What was that? as I hightailed it out of there.

I walked toward Josh, his expression growing more and more worried every step I took. I put one hand on his shoulder and said, "Boy. That was genius." His face changed on a dime. He smiled. "But don't you be hittin' me with no orange again."

40

"Genius?" Cully said. "Don't take no genius to smack you out." He laughed. "Bet it took you so long gettin' back here 'cause you went off to cry like a baby. Your face is red 'nough."

I spun around to Cully. "You better shut up or I'll smack the business out of you. I'm all red from runnin' up and down tryin' to find y'all."

Cully laughed again and took another dag of the cigarette. "Don't be kiddin' yourself. You ain't no match for me, No Good."

"You wanna prove that right now?"

We got closer and closer to each other.

"I'd hit you so hard your clothes won't fit," he told me.

"I'd hit you so hard you'd be nothin' but gator bait."

"I'd hit you so hard we'll have to change your name to Johnny No Face."

"I'd hit you so hard all the king's horses and all king's men would have to paste you back together again."

"I'd hit you so hard your daddy gonna have to get himself another orphan."

For some reason, Cully's last threat didn't set right with me. I paused as the impact of his comeback settled in. "You take that back."

"I ain't takin' nothin' back. You been dishin' it out just as much as me. If you can't take it, git out of the kitchen." He stuck the cigarette back in his mouth and gave me his know-it-all smirk.

When a guy gets to a point where there ain't nothing left to say, then he's got only one thing left to do. With that cigarette still hanging out the side of his lips, I threw Cully a punch straight to the mouth. The cigarette smashed against his cheek and he stumbled backwards, trying to wipe out the burning ash from his face.

"Hit him back, Cully!" called out Jacob.

"Yeah!" said Seth. "Right in the kisser!"

41

I shot a quick glance at Josh, hoping for some support on my side. But he just stood there like he didn't even know me. By the time I turned back to Cully, he was swinging that big fist of his straight into my face. I fell backwards and smacked the back of my head against a tree. I tried to get back upright, but Cully kept coming after me. Cully launched his next punch, but I spun around the tree so that his fist smacked the bark.

"Ah!" He grabbed his hand.

I swung my leg behind his and tripped him to the ground. Then I didn't waste a second. I kicked him in his ribs over and over again. He buckled and slid across the ground, but I kept coming at him. He grabbed my foot in the middle of a kick and twisted it around so much it felt like my foot was gonna pop right off. I hit the ground, and Cully jumped right on top of me. He hit me with a left, then a right, then a left, then a right. He was swinging at me like a wild man, hitting me in the chest, in the face, in the head. I flapped my arms in front of me trying to block the punches, but he kept finding a way around.

Then suddenly, he stopped. Still straddling me, he stared down at me, panting like he just run himself across the county. And in one breath, he gargled up a wad of spit and let it fly. The greenish glob smacked the middle of my face.

I twisted and wiped it clean.

Cully stood, still looking down at me. "You ain't nothin', No Good. Nothin'! Don't you ever be thinkin' you can take me. Next time I won't be so easy on you. You ain't nothin'."

I slid along the ground, backing away from him. Everyone stared at me.

Cully spun his back to me. "C'mon, Jacob and Seth. Let's get out of here." He walked past Josh, and for no reason, gave him a shove. "Scarecrow."

Josh stumbled but stopped himself from hitting the ground. Cully marched off with Jacob and Seth close behind.

After the three were out of sight and crossing the tracks, I sat up against a tree and silently pouted. Josh stared at me and then walked right up to me.

"What you want?" I kicked up some leaves like a little kid who just got a whuppin'.

Josh took a few steps back and stopped, still staring at me. And though I knew he was watching, I dropped my head in my hands and cried. It was a hot cry, the kind where it feels like fire is coming out. I pushed the tears away hard with my hands, but they just kept right on coming.

Soon, I realized it wasn't no use fighting. I stood up, still crying and sniffling. "Well…c'mon. Let's…get on home…"

I walked, wobbly knees and all. Josh followed me, but I didn't once look back at him. I kept my head down and went right on walking like I was all alone.

Five

Old Man Badeau

Back at home, I sat on my bed and opened my book The Adventures of Superman. I'd already read or otherwise thumbed through the well-worn red book about a hundred times, but I always liked reading it when I was upset. I had stopped crying long before reaching home, but I was still in no mood for doing much else.

I stared at one of the colored drawings in the middle of the book and in my mind replayed the story of the superhero that went along with it.

When I looked up, I saw Josh sitting in the chair at the corner of my room. He was staring at me.

"What the diddily you want?" I asked.

He didn't say nothin'. He just shrugged.

I looked back down at the book. "I ain't gonna do nothin' but read," I told him. I paused. "You can read too if ya want. Got books under m'bed." I paused again and then looked at him. Josh was still just sitting there staring at me. "You can read, can't ya?"

At first, Josh didn't do nothing. Then he shrugged like he didn't know what I was asking him.

"What do you mean you don't know. You either can or can't read. Which is it?"

"I know my ABC's."

"But you can't read?"

He turned away and shook his head real slow.

"Shoot, boy. What kinda brother I got stuck with? Even a moron can read. You're the real No Good in this family." I returned to my book, gripping it hard and angrily. I tried to read, but instead I just stared at the words like they were foreign. I could just feel Josh gazing at me with those cow eyes of his that were all pitiful and helpless like always. I wanted him to leave—just scoot on out the door. But he didn't budge an inch. He just sat there, not moving, not talking.

I was still fuming. I looked up from my book and opened my mouth to yell at him again, but stopped the minute I saw his face. It was all red and puffy with tears pouring down. He wasn't all-out crying since he wasn't moving or making noise; he was like a statue in the rain.

I dropped the book in my lap and my face melted. I went from hatred to pity in a heartbeat. Instead of feeling mad, I felt like a turd. I tried to speak. "I…"

But then Josh bolted out of my room like a jackrabbit.

I cursed under my breath. "Ah, fiddlesticks…" I jumped out of bed and followed him.

He stopped on the front porch, sort of leaning against a support like he couldn't stand up without it. I let the screen door slam behind me and stood back, watching him. This time, he was crying good and hard. I could barely hear him, but his body shook and he occasionally wiped the snot from his face.

A moist evening breeze was settling in, kicking up leaves and dirt, and dark clouds overhead were rolling in. I could smell the damp musk swirling in the air. It was fixing to rain any second.

45

I stepped up to Josh and put a hand on his back. He jerked his shoulder, making it clear that he didn't want none of me. I stood there feeling as helpless as a one-legged dog. What can I do? I thought. It ain't my fault the boy can't read.

I stepped on over to the opposite railing and looked down the street as fat raindrops smacked the road's hard-packed white sand. A couple houses down, I could see Old Man Jones waddling across his yard with his hands over his head, making his way to his front porch. The sound of rain slapping the trees and wood-shingled roof felt calming, like it always did during a quiet Florida summer shower. I remembered when I was little kid, coming out to the porch and waiting out Momma's crying fits about not having any babies. I'd listen to the rain and pretend I somehow brought a little brother home and made Momma and everybody happy. Don't know how I got this little brother; I just brought him home like I found him out in the woods.

As I thought about this little daydream, I came to realize how stupid it was and I was glad I ain't never told Cully about it.

Without turning my head, I said, "You ain't no good, Josh. I didn't mean it." I waited for him to say something back, but he just kept on standing there crying. "You know, sometimes I just say things. Don't mean nothin' by it; they just words. Nothin' else." I waited again, and again nothing. "Wouldn't say nothin' to tweak your fence. I mean, not on purpose. 'Cause I…" I turned to him. "…I always wanted a li—" I stopped the moment I realized what I was about to say.

Josh rubbed more snot away and turned to me. "Wanted what?"

I looked at those cow eyes of his and his red face and suddenly felt all choked up. I turned away from him and blurted out, "Shoot, boy. It ain't the end of the world if ya can't read."

I heard a stomping on the porch, and I turned back just in time to see Josh running off into the rain.

"Wha— Josh!" I called out, but he just kept right on running down the street as the rain kept coming down harder and harder.

I thought about chasing after him, but I knew Pa was on his way home for lunch, and he'd be wantin' to eat right away and not wait on a couple boys gallivanting around in the rain. At just that moment, I saw Pa jogging down the road from opposite way Josh ran. He had his head down, using a newspaper like an umbrella; he probably hadn't seen Josh take off.

Pa jumped up onto the porch with his awkward limp and shook off the rain. Before I could open my mouth, he said, "Boy, what happened to you?"

It took me a beat to realize that he was probably talkin' about my swollen face. I touched my left cheek. After making Josh run off, I'd forgotten about my fight with Cully. "Got in a fight."

He stepped up closer to me. "I can see that. But what happened?"

"Cully was talkin' smack."

He pointed at my face. "Your best friend did that to you?"

I didn't know what to say, so I dropped my head.

"Boy, now I know Cully, and I know how he talks smack, but words don't make your face look like a busted melon. In fact, I bet you threw the first punch."

I looked at Pa but then turned away.

Pa shook his head. "Boy, one of these days you got to learn to use your head and mouth to git out of a corner. 'Cause today I can see you lost that fight with Cully. And I don't mean you lost it because you look like a punching bag; you lost it the moment you threw that first punch. Now, I know you can talk and at times you can even think; you just gotta use them tools when you backed into a corner. Ya hear?"

I nodded.

47

"Okay. Now get yourself inside and wash that face up before Momma sees you. She ain't as understanding 'bout these things."

I hesitated, searching out into the rain.

"Well, what you waitin' for?"

"Josh."

"Josh?" He looked around the porch as if trying to find him. He turned back to me. "Where he at?"

"He crazy. He run off in the rain."

Pa's eyes got all dark, and he took a step toward me.

"I didn't do nothin'. He just run himself off."

"That boy didn't just run off for no reason without you being involved. You dare him or somethin'?"

"I didn't dare him. I didn't do nothin'."

"Well, you better get on out there and find that boy before Momma has lunch ready, or she'll be smackin' two backsides good and raw. Git!"

Pa gave me a good shove out into the downpour and I fell into a sprint, not sure where I was going to end up. Down the street a few houses, I ended up at Cully's.

I stood on his porch and shook off the rain. Facing his front door, I thought about seeing Cully again. No doubt he'd laugh at my swollen face and talk smack, and then we'd be fighting all over again. I turned toward the street and thought about Momma and her wooden spoon. I couldn't go back, but I didn't want to stay neither. By the time I turned back around, the front door was open. It was Jeannie.

She leaned against the door frame and looked at me, bored. She wasn't wearing much: barefoot, cut-off shirt, and panties. "Cully ain't here."

"Good."

"Good?"

I straightened up. "Uh…I came over to…uh, is Josh here?"

48

"Uh? Josh who?" Jeannie stepped out and closed the door.

"My brother, Josh."

"You ain't got no brother."

"He an orphan from First Baptist. So is Josh here or what?"

Jeannie stepped up next to me and leaned against a post. She stared me down. "I ain't seen no Josh. Just me. Me and that old fart in there."

I looked out into the rain, trying to think where Josh could be. "Okay. Bye, Jeannie."

"Wait. No Good?"

I turned.

"Uh…" She looked at me like she was trying to read words on my face. "I hope you find him."

I nodded, took a breath, and ran off. But this time I made up my mind where I was going. I headed straight down the Stink Bug Trail to where we had stolen Old Man Badeau's clothes the day before.

I got to a bush at the edge of the small clearing where we'd spotted Old Man Badeau. I tried to find cover from the stupid rain. Down on my belly, I crawled underneath a low pair of palm fronds and looked toward Lake Monroe. I couldn't see nothin' but a gray wall of rain. As I lay there, I could feel the water seeping through my pants and into my shoes. The wetter I got, the less it bothered me, but I didn't feel like staying there forever. Plus Momma was gonna be stomping mad across the porch any second wondering where we ran off to. I stood and ran back up the Stink Bug Trail.

By now, the rain had made a fast-moving creek down the center of the path, so I hopped back and forth from root to root to avoid the water. On one hop, I slipped on a root and fell backwards, landing butt-first into about two inches of water that splashed through my pants as if I had a garden hose going through it. I tried to get up quick, but I slipped again, this time smacking the back of my head against another root and rolling face-down into the creek. I got up and coughed out the nasty, muddy water from my mouth and nose.

"You all right, boy?" The voice was so deep and piercing that for a heartbeat I thought it was God himself.

I shot right up and spun around, nearly slipping again on the slick waterslide still splashing at my feet.

I couldn't tell where the voice had come from until it spoke again. "You can come over here, if you want. Out of that rain."

I stepped between a gap of bushes and in front of me was Old Man Badeau himself, sitting on a log, looking dry as can be. Above him was a rusted sheet of metal with a faded logo of Borden's Elsie the Cow facing down. It rested on a bunch of branches and sticks. Big rain drops hit the metal from tree leaves above it like marbles plinking the walls of a shed.

I stepped into Old Man Badeau's fort and saw he wasn't alone. To my left, sitting on another log facing him was Josh. Mud and water drizzled down his arms and head, and his face was beet-red. He didn't look at all pleased to see me.

The roof wasn't tall enough for me to stand upright, so I headed over as far away from the two as I could and sat down on the ground. I shook and hugged myself to ward off the cold.

Old Man Badeau spoke. "Why you kids be runnin' 'round in the rain when you gots roofs over your heads is beyond me. Make no sense."

I looked Old Man Badeau over. He was a broad man with huge forearms and shoulders; probably the strongest man I'd ever seen. He was wearing a pale-blue collared shirt and tan pants, both of which appeared a couple sizes too small, and he was barefoot. His hair was puffed out like a globe with streaks of gray and black. He had scars on his face and one long, deep scar that ran up one arm from his wrist to his bicep.

My shivering got worse the longer I sat there on the ground. I could feel the splashing of rain on my back, but I was too cold to move. I saw that Josh was shivering too, but he was so focused on me that the cold didn't seem to bother him one inch.

Old Man Badeau reached into his pocket and pulled out a handkerchief and held it out to me. "Dry off that face," he ordered.

I took the handkerchief and wiped my face down. The handkerchief stunk like piss and I took a good look at it. It was the same handkerchief Josh had swiped from Old Man Badeau the other day. I looked at Josh and he was still staring me down, which struck me as odd. Seemed like anytime I talked to Josh directly or had a beef with him, he'd just turn away or keep his head down. Now, it didn't faze him a bit to stare at me straight on. I briefly wondered if maybe Old Man Badeau did have magic.

Old Man Badeau held out his hand and I passed the handkerchief back to him. He snatched it away and stuck it back into his pocket. It occurred to me then that Pa had the same kind of tan pants...and the same baby-blue shirt. It weren't so unusual to see another man with the same clothes as my Pa, but I ain't never seen a Negro with same kind of clothes unless they were all torn and beat up; the clothes Old Man Badeau had on were good as new. They didn't quite fit, but they were good as new.

It didn't take me another second to figure this out. I glared over at Josh, ready to tell him off for giving away Pa's clothes to a Negro. But Josh's death stare stopped me cold.

"You two don't get dry soon," Old Man Badeau said, "you gonna catch yo' death. How come you'ins 'round these woods anyhow?" His voice was so deep and booming, it sounded like he was talking through a hollow log.

I didn't dare speak. As much as I didn't believe all that voodoo flibbertygibbet Cully was always shelling out, I didn't want to take any chances neither. I figured it was better to believe it just enough.

51

I looked at Josh, and for once he wasn't staring at me. He faced Old Man Badeau and shrugged.

"Don't know?" Old Man Badeau turned to me. "What about you? You don't know, neither? Eh? Not speakin'? You know I ain't no bogeyman."

I lifted my eyebrows in surprise.

"I know. I hear what you kids be whisperin' 'bout me every time I come 'round. Bogeyman Badeau what dey call me." He emitted a strange sound from his mouth, like a phlegmy puff of air. "Kids," he said.

For as long as I'd been alive, I'd never heard of Bogeyman Badeau. But it didn't sound like a half-bad name for the old Negro.

Old Man Badeau leaned off to one side and peered up at the darkening rain clouds. The rain seemed to have lightened up a pinch, but it was still coming down good and plenty. The old Negro straightened and said, "'Bout another thirty minutes or so left in dem clouds. You two lucky it jist an evenin' stowm. Not one of dem tropical stowms that'll knock ya down like a dead dawg. You ain't never seen a stowm 'til you stuck in one of dem."

The man cleared out his throat and spat a wad of phlegm off to one side. He rattled snot around in his sinuses and let out another spit.

"What I'd do fo' some snuff." He turned to me. "You ain't got some of you pappy's tobacco on ya, do ya?"

I shook my head.

"Good. Kids you age shouldn't be doin' dat stuff anyhow. You'll wind up an old fool like me." He rubbed his nose, snorted, and let out another wad of phlegm to the ground. He looked back and forth between Josh and me. "If I didn't know no better, I'd say you two'ins wanna tear into each otha', somethin' fierce." He swung his hand back and forth from Josh to me, and then stopped at Josh. "You got it in fo' him, boy?"

Josh turned to me with his dead stare again and then back to Old Man Badeau.

The man smiled. "So what'd he do? Or what'd you do to him? C'mon. We got time waitin' out the storm. What's da beef?"

Josh turned back to me, shook his head, and said, "Nothin'."

The man grunted. "Boy, I got m'self in a heap of trouble for nothin' before. Nothin' could slap yo' hide in jail fasta than green grass through a goose. If I learned one thing in my life it's you take care you nothin's before they become somethin'. You understand, boy?"

The more Old Man Badeau spoke, the more confused I got. It wasn't so much what he said, but how he said it. He wasn't like I imagined him at all. I mean, I wasn't expecting no devil man like Cully talked him up, but I wasn't expecting this neither. He sounded just like Pa. He was already dressing like Pa with them tan pants and baby-blue shirt; now he was talking like him. He certainly didn't sound like no Negro I ever heard. But of course, I never once sat and talked to a Negro before. Usually just heard them yelling and cursing at us after taking some fruit.

Old Man Badeau turned to me. "So what 'bout you? What nothin' you didn't do to him?"

Josh turned to me all mean-looking, and the old man started staring down at me just like Pa. I opened my mouth to speak but nothing really came. "I...Well, I..."

"What? Speak up, boy. Can't hardly hear you with all the rain smacking m'roof."

I went to speak again, but then stopped. I closed my mouth, gathered my thoughts, and then started over. "I just said stuff I didn't mean, that's all. And this boy just took off like lightning. I told him it didn't mean nothin'. Just said it, that's all."

Old Man Badeau shook his head. "That's all it takes, boy. That's all it takes. Now you got your best friend gunning to kill you."

"He ain't my friend." I paused, realizing how what I said sounded. "I mean, he's my brother."

Badeau looked surprised. "Your brother?" He looked at Josh as if sizing him up.

I explained, "We picked him up from First Baptist."

The old man nodded his head real slow like he understood. "Um." He turned back to me and said, "You think just 'cause he's family now, you can walk all over him? I tell you, family don't deserve that, no sir. Family come first, in my book. Always."

Once again, I opened my big mouth and said something I shouldn't have. "But you ain't got no family." I knew it the instant I said it. I scooted back and squinted, preparing myself for a wallop.

But instead, all I got was silence.

Old Man Badeau sat back on his log and breathed out slowly, a kind of breathing where I could tell his mind was trudging back two or three times further than I'd been alive.

After a long while of no one saying a word, Old Man Badeau spoke. And when he did, he spoke slow and low, like an old, old man. "That ain't all true." There was a story behind them words, for sure. Josh and I sat there looking at the old Negro, waiting to hear the rest of it come out, but he didn't go no further. He just left it hanging over us like those heavy drops pelting the sheet metal.

Before I could tell myself to keep quiet, I went right on talking. "Well, if you got family, how come you livin' out here?"

Old Man Badeau took another one of them deep breaths, looked away, and then looked up at me. "Boy, you jist don't know how to keep that mouth of yours shut. No wonder Josh wants to smack you' head in."

I turned to Josh. He was gazing at Old Man Badeau, and for once I could see a bit of a smile creep across his face. It made me feel better to not see Josh scowling. I turned back to Old Man Badeau before Josh caught me looking at him.

The man stared deep at me, his head angled forward and his eyes up, causing his forehead to wrinkle like a turtle's neck. He took a breath again and said, "I got myself a grandson. He 'bout your age, in fact. And I love him. I do. But…but there's jist some things that you jist can't fix. But I tell you, as God as my witness, if I could do somethin' to fix things, I would." He sat upright. "Sure would."

We waited out the next several minutes in silence. The rain lightened and the incessant roar of the tapping leaves quieted to tiny scattered splashes.

Old Man Badeau leaned to one side and looked up at the clouds. "It's breakin' up." Leaning back to us, he pointed to the side. "You two best be headin' home. You momma and pappy prob'ly havin' a fit."

No doubt he was dead center. I looked at Josh, and his eyes were sayin' You ready? I turned back to Old Man Badeau. Felt like saying something, but I realized I hadn't said nothin' right all day. So I just stood up and headed out. Josh followed right behind.

A little ways down the trail, I threw a glance over my shoulder and caught the back of Old Man Badeau's puffy black and gray hair. I turned forward and kept right on walking.

As soon as we came out of the Stink Bug Trail, I turned to Josh. "We best run from here. We already late as sin."

But Josh replied with, "He an orphan too."

I did myself a double-take. "What?" I turned back toward the woods. "You mean Old Man Badeau? He ain't no orphan." Then I realized that Old Man Badeau musta had a momma and pa once too. I guess everyone does.

I could see in Josh's face that Old Man Badeau being an orphan was right important. I didn't try to understand. But I

55

knew that I'd said enough to Josh for one day that weren't right. So I just said, "Yeah. Guess you're right." Then I nodded down the street. "C'mon. Let's hightail it."

*   *   *

As expected, we took a beatin' and missed out on lunch when we got back home. For dinner, we had to eat the old, stale sandwiches Momma'd made us for lunch while Momma and Pa ate a big ol' chicken dinner that looked so good I about broke down crying.

That night, Josh and I lay in bed, me with my stomach growling, listening to the crickets and smelling the musk of rain the evening sun kicked into the air. Josh's skinny foot and arm rubbed against me, and both felt as cold as a dead rat.

I got up, yanked out a wool blanket from under the bed, and threw it out over Josh's side. I settled back down.

"Thanks, Johnny," whispered Josh.

I closed my eyes and whispered back, "Ain't no thing, Josh. Ain't no thing."

Six

Tommy J

I jumped out of bed to the sound of commotion. I could hear Ansel's momma screaming outside. Anyone could pick out her voice; she talked like her neck was all twisted, and her screams were ten times as bad. I had to give the bed a good couple bounces to wake up Josh.

"What?" Josh said, all groggy-like.

"Git up, Josh, and git some clothes on! Something's goin' wrong out by Old Man Jones's house."

"What?" Josh sat up. "What's going on?"

I put on my clothes as I talked. "I don't know. But we gonna miss it if we don't get our butts out of bed."

I opened my bedroom door and saw Momma pacing down the hallway with a handkerchief up to her lips. Her face was all red and wet with tears. She was still in her nightgown, but she was walkin' so fast, it was obvious she'd been up a while.

"Momma, what—?"

"Oh, no you don't." She marched right up to me. "Don't you leave that room, you two. You two still grounded, and I don't want you to be messing around with all this goin' on and a killer on the loose."

"A what? A killer? What happened, Momma?"

"Jist get yourself in that room, No Good. I don't want you leaving Josh's side. You hear me?"

She about knocked me backwards as she slammed the bedroom door in my face.

Stunned, I spun around. Josh was hopping around on one foot trying to pull on his pants. "What's goin' on, Johnny?"

I shook my head. "I don't know. But I'll be a monkey's uncle if we ain't gonna find out."

I headed to the window and worked it open. The windows in my house were a good fifty pounds, and the only way to keep them open was to wedge something sideways underneath. "Josh. Fetch me a book," I said as I struggled with it.

"Book? Which book?"

"Next to the…bed," I grunted. "Get a big one."

Josh grabbed me a book. "This?"

I gave it a quick glance as I continued jiggling the window up. "No! Bigger!"

Josh swapped it out with the biggest book on the floor next to my bed. "This?"

"Yeah! Jam it up under the window. And quick!"

Josh squeezed underneath me and jammed the book in. I nodded and let go of the window. It let out a squeak and then came down with a "Thunk!" onto the book. But the book held.

I caught my breath and turned to Josh. "Good. You ready?" He nodded. "Alright. C'mon."

I squeezed under the window and plopped outside. I stood up and turned back to Josh. "C'mon. And careful of the book. Don't knock it out."

Josh slid out and thunked to the ground.

"C'mon." We ran. "We'll go the long way so no one sees," I whispered loudly.

It was dark, real dark. The sun wasn't going to be headin' up for another hour, and there wasn't a star in the sky. It was the sort of sky that looked all swallowed up, like a cave when you ain't got a lantern. The only light was coming from the houses, and it wasn't much. Just enough to be spooky.

We headed up and around a patch of woods that lined the back of the houses down our street. I signaled Josh to stay low. I stood behind a tree and peeked around. I could see the back and side of Old Man Jones's house. It was crawling with adults standing and talking and walking every which way, ladies in nightgowns and shirtless men. I could see Officer Carter yelling at a group of folks that they were getting too close. In the group, I could see Cully in his underdrawers hopping up and down, trying to see past the army of adults. From where I was at, I couldn't get a good look at what Cully was trying to see.

I worked around the other side of the tree and could see the back of Ansel's house, next door to Old Man Jones's.

"What you seein'?" whispered Josh.

I ducked back behind the tree. "I can't see nothin' from here. But I know where we can go. C'mon!"

We headed a little farther down and came out of the woods just behind Ansel's house. I ran up to the side of the house where Ansel's mom had put up one of them fancy lattices.

"This thing ain't too strong," I said to Josh. "Wait 'til I'm up it, then you start."

"We climbing this?"

"How else we gonna get on Ansel's roof?"

I started on up and I could feel the rickety old thing snap and whine the whole way. At the top, I swung my legs around and hopped on the slanted roof. I looked back over the side and called out, "C'mon, Josh!"

Josh took forever getting up. I kept a lookout. The crowd of people at Old Man Jones's house was on the other side of Ansel's house, but who was to say that one of them couldn't wander their way over here.

Josh reached the top and I whispered, "Take my hand." I helped him up and over the edge of the roof. "C'mon. And watch your step. It's slipperier up here than the Stink Bug Trail."

We crept along the back side of the roof, all bent over like Old Man Jones with a backache. We couldn't see what we were steppin' on, though I could feel sticks and small rocks rolling around under my feet. All I could think about was sliding off the side of the roof and how ticked Momma would be if she found out I'd broken my head. The roof's angle kept us hidden from the front of the house, but our crunching footsteps were loud. I winced with every step.

Just before we reached the peak of the roof, I got down on my belly and with a wave of my hand told Josh to do the same. We crawled the last couple feet and peered over the top of the roof down onto the mess of people. Many of them had lanterns or army flashlights, lighting up the side of the house bright enough to see everything.

Just past the crowd, I could see Officer Carter and a few other cops pushing back the crowds. Behind him was Old Man Jones's house. The house was all wood, standing on stacks of cinderblocks, like most all other houses down our street. In the gap that separated the bottom of the house from the muddy ground, I could see Tommy J's body sticking out. His dead body, that is.

My eyes opened wide and I sucked in my breath and held it good and tight. In all the talking and yelling and commotion that woke me up and in all of Momma's sniffling telling me to stay in my room, I ain't never would have guessed in a million years that I was going to see what I saw.

My heart fluttered inside my chest and my mind shot out in a gajillion directions all at once. It took a full minute for my brain to make sense of it all.

No doubt it's Tommy J. He's lying on his back with his bony legs sugar white, spotted in brown and red. And he's as dead as they come.

That's all my mind would say.

"Who's that?" whispered Josh.

It took me a second to catch my breath. "That's Tommy J. No doubt."

"What happen to him?"

I shook my head and my voice rattled. "Don't know. But I done seen enough. C'mon, Josh."

We headed back on down the roof and through the woods to my bedroom window. But when we got there, that book we stuck in the opening had popped right out and the window was closed. Both Josh and I tried to work the stupid window back up, but it wouldn't budge.

"C'mon Josh," I said like a whipped horse. "Let's face the beatin'."

We headed on around to the front of the house. When we walked up the porch and opened the door, there was Momma—standing right there like she was expecting us. Her face at first registered surprise, but immediately turned to rage.

I don't know what it was, exactly, but something came over me all of a sudden. And whether I wanted to or not, I started crying. Right there on the porch, in full view of Momma, Josh, and the whole world behind me. Tears fell like a rainstorm.

This caught Momma off guard mighty good. She opened her mouth to talk, but then went speechless.

Not knowing how to stop crying, I stepped inside and said, "Momma..." and fell into Momma's arms like a little baby.

Momma wrapped her arms around and patted me.

I barely got out, "I didn't even like Tommy J," and then I kept right on crying.

In a voice that I hadn't heard since I was about three years old, Momma said to me, "Now, now...you ain't got nothin' to cry 'bout, No Good. You okay." She dug her fingers into my back, givin' it a good scratch; Momma always did this to calm me down. Then she pulled away from me and looked into my eyes. "Why don't you go on and wash those tears in the sink," she said, "and head on back to bed. Momma will be there in a moment."

And like a three-year-old, I walked past her and followed her orders to the T.

I laid in bed staring at the ceiling and wiping my tears away, expectin' any minute for Josh to come in and lie beside me. But he never came. He sure enough had seen me bawling in my Momma's arms like I was an infant and had heard Momma tell me to go back to bed. I couldn't help but wonder what that boy thought of me, all that crying. I didn't even know what to think of it.

I closed my eyes and the only thing I could see was Tommy J. But I fell asleep anyhow.

Seven

Now What?

I woke up all sorts of confused. Josh wasn't there and the sun was shining good and bright through the window. I stood up and my head spun in circles. I thought about the sneaking around Josh and I did earlier that morning and about seeing Tommy J, and I wondered if I had just dreamt it all. I rubbed my face and let out a good belch.

I staggered into the hallway and the house was empty and quiet. I headed into the kitchen and stopped when I saw Josh sitting there at the table. He looked up at me from his plate of half-eaten day-old biscuits and smiled.

"Hi," he said.

"Where's Momma?"

He shrugged and swiveled his head back and forth like he was lookin' for her. "Dunno."

I sat down next to Josh. "That the last of the biscuits?"

Josh nodded and pushed the plate to me. I took a bite out of one of them and surveyed Josh while I chewed. I thought about the crying I'd done, and I hated myself for letting him see

63

me like that. He'd seen me the day before, after I fought with Cully, but shedding tears after being walloped in the face weren't nothin' like cryin' when you ain't got blood dripping out of you.

I swallowed the biscuit and said, "You ain't gonna tell no one."

Josh stopped chewing and frowned at me. "Tell 'em what?"

"You know what I'm talkin' about. What I did. When we came back home."

Josh looked at me like I was growing antlers, and I wondered again if I had dreamt it after all.

"You mean the cryin'?"

I didn't say nothin'. I just kept looking at him.

Then Josh smiled at me, and I felt like sluggin' the boy. But before I moved, he said, "'Long as you don't say nothin' about us bathin' naked together."

. All at once, I could breathe again. I smiled and put my hand on Josh's shoulder. "Josh...sometimes, you alright."

He smiled and took another bite of biscuit.

I reached for more food when something occurred to me. "So..." I turned to him. "...you liked swingin' your gingerbread around my face?"

Josh laughed and shook his head. "Na. Just nobody gotta know about it, that's all."

"That's for darn sure."

Pa came walking in through the kitchen door with a couple of men behind him. Without breaking step, he said, "No Good. Josh. You two get your shoes on, pack some clothes for tomorrow, and head on over to Cully's with Miss Maples." Just as he said it, in come Miss Maples through the door behind the men.

"To Cully's?" I asked.

"Don't be fussin' me, boy. Now do what I said."

Pa had a tone that let me know he meant business. I nudged Josh, grabbed the biscuit, and headed off to my room. Josh followed. Along the way, I pulled out a potato sack from the closet in the hall. I stuffed the sack with tomorrow's clothes for Josh and me and then sat on my bed and wiggled on my shoes. I looked to find Josh staring at me.

"You heard Pa. Put your shoes on."

Josh hesitated. "He mad at us?"

"Na. But he's up in a huff 'bout somethin'. No doubt it's got do do with Tommy J. Now, put your shoes on before he whups us raw."

Josh was slower than a monkey figurin' out a telephone. "C'mon, boy," I said when he finally got his shoes on.

We headed down the road to Cully's. Miss Maples was waiting for us on the porch and followed us step for step like we were criminals. When we got to the front door, I went to knock, but Miss Maples reached over me and knocked really fast.

For the first time in my entire life, Cully's grandpappy answered the door himself. He was in his dirty, nasty long johns and was holding a rifle 'bout as decrepit and rusty as him. The man was at least seventy years old, but he could've been a hundred for all I knew. I was told that he had built this house by hand when Cully's daddy was a little boy, but by the time I met him, he was the crustiest man I knew.

"Mmmm. You Maple?" He talked like he had a mouthful of tobacco.

"Yes, yes. Excuse me. Let the children in. Excuse me."

Miss Maples talked Yankee but dressed like a plantation owner's wife and smelled like tapioca and sweat. She was one of them adults who never spoke to children. In fact, it wouldn't have surprised me one iota if she was fluffy-dressed, big-haired, and elderly the day she popped out of her momma. Seeing her at Cully's house was like seeing a queen in a mud pit.

Miss Maples tiptoed around Josh and me and made her way into the house in front of us. Cully's grandpappy watched her as she wiggled around the furniture, afraid to touch anything.

The old man then turned back to Josh and me. "Mmmm. Watcha gunna stand there all dee fer? Mmmm. Git on in."

I liked watching Cully's grandpappy talk. He was always movin' his jaw this way and that with every word.

Josh and I stepped inside and stood in the middle of Cully's living room as we watched poor Miss Maples sneak around like she was trying not to step on a landmine. Miss Maples finally decided on a chair along the wall. She patted it with a handkerchief that she took out of her pocket and then sat down real slow.

Cully's grandpappy stepped up behind us, still holding the rifle in his hand. "Mmmm. Don't sit there. That's the dawg's chair."

"Well, the dog can sit elsewhere while I'm here," replied Miss Maples. "Chairs are intended for humans, after all."

"Mmmm..." Cully's grandpappy tilted his head. "The dawg pisses on it."

"Eeeekkk!"

Miss Maples sprung up so fast, she 'bout flew across the room. Josh and I couldn't help but slip out a few chuckles.

Miss Maples wiped the back of her dress with her handkerchief. "Well...well...I'm...I'm off to the kitchen to make some tea. I must have my tea. Where do you keep...never mind. I'll figure it out on my own." As she strutted off, she waved the handkerchief in front of her. "Phew...phew..."

With Miss Maples out of the room, Josh and I turned to Cully's grandpappy. He gave a few munches on his gums and then said, "Mmmm. Headin' off to nap. Don't no one go nowhere."

We watched Cully's grandpappy shuffle through the house with his rifle. The back of his nasty long johns was flapped open, and we got a full view of his wrinkled backside as he disappeared down the hallway.

Josh tapped my shoulder. "Where's Cully?" he asked.

Before I could shrug my shoulders, the front door opened and in walked Cully and Jeannie.

Jeannie was in the middle of some sort of hissy, but I didn't hear enough to figure out what she was mad about.

It wasn't until they closed the door that they noticed Josh and me. Cully was the first to speak, "What you here for?"

This was the first time Cully and I seen each other since we'd fought, and I could tell by his tone that he coulda gone longer before seeing me again.

"Pa told us we had to head on over here with Miss Maples," I said.

"Miss Maples?" Jeannie said. "That old hag comin' to our house?"

A clattering of pots and pans arose from the next room.

"She's in the kitchen," Josh spoke up.

"No bologna," Cully said.

Miss Maples emerged. "That kitchen is horrendous. I— Ah, you two are here. I was assigned to watch over you children until which time I am relieved or otherwise you are released from my oversight. In the meantime, you are to be in my care and follow the rules that I set. Rule one: no—"

"Who the diddly you think you are?" Jeannie said. "Miss Stick-Up-The-Butt?"

"I beg your—"

"I ain't listenin' to nobody tell me nothin'! I'm gettin' out." Jeannie turned to leave, but stopped. She looked at me. Then she turned toward the door and gave it a good hard frown. Then she turned back to me and said, "I'll be in the bedroom!"

With the slam of Jeannie and Cully's bedroom door, Miss Maples kept right on talkin' like the girl hadn't said a word. "Rule one: no leaving the premises. Rule two…"

"Leavin' where?" Cully asked.

"The premises," she repeated.

"Prema…" Cully started. "We ain't got no prem-a-sists!"

"I mean no leaving…this house." Miss Maples snuffed her nose. "Rule two: no screaming or running about while I take my morning meditation or my early afternoon catnap or anytime when I'm reading or reflecting quietly. Rule three: you'll have to fend for yourself for food. That kitchen is a…" She shivered. "And rule f—"

"When do we leave?" I asked.

Miss Maples stared down her nose at me. "Rule four:" she continued, "I ask the questions. Understood? Good. I'll be…" She looked around. "I'll be reading on…the back porch." She tiptoed past us and made her way out the back door and closed it with a slam.

At first, Cully, Josh, and I just stood there staring at the back door, trying to figure out what was goin' on. But then Josh giggled and said, "Miss Stick-Up-The-Crotch."

Cully and I laughed and looked at each other. The instant we made eye contact, both of us stopped laughing. Cully stood there staring at me and then said, "This is a pile o' crock. I'm headin' out."

He turned and marched right on out the front door and slammed it shut.

Alone in the living room, Josh and I took a look around. Of all the years I'd known Cully, I'd barely ever gone inside his house. It was just one of those things. We were good friends, but inside his house was out of bounds. It wasn't nothin' he was proud of, plus Cully wasn't the type to be locked up inside all day anyhow.

The house was cold and felt like a stranger's. Standing there, I realized that I probably felt about the same as Josh had the past few days, all out of place.

Josh turned to me. "Now, whatta we do?"

I shook my head. "I don't know, Josh. I just—"

Before I could finish, the front door flew open and Cully came in flyin'. He crashed on the floor and bounced into a sideways roll. Looming in the doorway was Cully's pa, whom I almost never saw. He was a huge man, 'bout six and a half feet, all muscle, bald, and forever looked mad. He had one of them wrinkled creases on his face in the shape of a frown.

Cully's pa pointed at Cully who was still all curled up on the floor like a kitten. "You stay in here with ya sister, ya hear? If I catch you once outside, I'll put a beatin' in ya so good you'll wish you weren't alive!"

He slammed the door so hard, the whole house rattled and clouds of dust plumed everywhere. A coupla seconds later, Miss Maples come shuffling in from the back.

"What on Earth was…are you two fist-fighting? Rule five: no fighting."

Cully sprang up from the floor. "No Good couldn't knock me down if he used a fifty-pound mallet. We weren't fightin'!"

"Then what…?"

"Pa jist came on by to make sure you were doin' your job, and you weren't, ya old bag! So why don't ya jist go on back out there and keep on not doin' your job."

I can't say that I ever liked Miss Maples much, but I wouldn't never talk to her like that. I always left it up to Cully to say the things that no one else would say.

Miss Maples shook her finger at Cully. "Now you listen here, young man. Children should not be speaking to adults so rudely. I will not put up with it. If you cannot follow a few simple rules then…"

69

"Then what?" Cully spat. "You ain't gonna do nothin'! You jist a busybody who can't keep your nose out, and watchin' us is the only job Daddy could give you since you useless doin' anything else." Cully walked past Josh and me, stepped out to the back porch, and slammed the door shut.

Miss Maples was speechless. She stood staring down the hall as if Cully was still there sassin' her. Then all at once, she let out another huff and tiptoed back into the kitchen.

Josh turned to me. "Now, whatta we do?"

"Josh," I said, putting my hand on his shoulder, "there ain't nothin' we can do but wait out this snot storm."

*　　*　　*

'Bout an hour later, Josh and I sat on the nasty couch in the middle of Cully's living room, more bored than a corpse on a fishing trip. There weren't a whole lot to look at: A peddle sewing machine along one wall with a picture of FDR above it. A small table along another wall with a pile of dirty clothes on top. An old radio about the size of a grown man. A hat rack in one corner with a couple of straw hats covered with so much dust, they looked like they hadn't been touched long before I was born. Another corner held a whole mess of shovels and rakes and hoes and sickles and other broken poles and sticks. They were all covered in dirt and clay but probably hadn't been touched since them hats were worn. The whole room, in fact, seemed lifeless and dead, like there weren't no one even living here. It didn't take but a minute of sitting on that rank couch to realize why I hadn't never come in Cully's house and why Cully didn't want to stay inside anyhow. It didn't feel like nobody's home.

"Ah, man," I finally let out. "I ain't gonna sit here and do nothin'."

I got up, headed over to the radio, and started fiddling with the knobs until I got it to light up. I waited for somethin'

70

to happen after the light came on, but nothin' did. I tinkered with some of the other knobs until a humming sound like something shaking inside came blaring out. I backed up a step and bumped into Josh.

"You try the volume?" asked Josh.

"I tried the volume."

I stepped forward and was about to turn another knob when the humming turned into a whistlin'. It was a pair of whistlin' tones that both grew louder real fast. The pair met up and made a terrible racket, louder than a screaming monkey.

Josh and I put our hands over our ears.

Then we both attacked the radio. Our hands went crazy. We twisted and turned and pushed every knob to try to stop the noise.

"Hit somethin'!" Josh said.

"I'm tryin'! I'm tryin'!"

POP! It sounded like an air rifle just let out.

Josh and I jumped back and fell into the couch. We both laid there with our eyes closed, waitin' for an explosion or somethin'. But there was just silence. Slowly, I opened my eyes. Standing next to the radio was Cully. He was holding a gnarly-looking power cord in one hand, dangling like a dead rat.

Miss Maples stepped up from behind the couch. "What on Earth was that?"

Cully tossed the cord to the ground. "Boy, you crazy or something? This piece of turkey dung hadn't worked since Momma was alive. Ain't no wonder they call you No Good."

"And I told you not to touch anything," Miss Maples added.

Cully glared at the lady like they were about to have it out again. But before anyone spoke, Miss Maples wheeled around and retreated to the kitchen.

I sat up. "How we supposed to know you got a busted radio? We ain't got nothin' to do but sit here and stare at each other."

71

"Don't I know it? I don't wanna be lookin' at you all day neither." Cully sat on a wooden crate near the radio, making it creak under his weight. Without saying nothin', he moved his eyes up and down the room, like he was waiting for something to happen.

I turned to Josh. He was still in the same position he was in when the radio popped. He gave me an expectant look, like he was waiting for me to say or do something.

I turned back to Cully. "So what're we gonna do?"

Cully sat up all angry. Then he slouched down, just as deflated as I was.

Then, all unexpected-like, Josh popped up and said, "I know what we do!"

Eight

Run Off

Cully and I sat up, surprised. We looked at each other, then I turned to Josh.

"What?" I asked.

Josh smiled and said to Cully, "Your bedroom got a window?"

"'Course it do."

"On the side of the house?"

Cully frowned at me. "W'cha got in mind, boy?" he asked Josh.

Without replying, Josh bounced right off the couch and shot down the hallway. Cully and I followed the skinny boy. Josh stopped at a closed door.

"That's Grandpappy and Pa's room, dummy," said Cully. "Jeannie and mine's the next." Cully pushed his way around Josh and opened up his bedroom door. Josh and I followed him in.

"Whacha want?" Jeannie barked as she sat up in bed, a magazine in her hands.

73

Josh headed toward the window, but Cully pushed him away.

"Hold your britches," Cully said. "You ain't gonna be jumpin' out that window 'lessin you tell me what it is you headin' off to."

Josh stared at Cully for a long while, a timid expression on his face. When he finally spoke, it was like he couldn't get the words out. "Uh… Old… Old Man Badeau." He cringed like he just said a naughty word.

Cully took a step back. "Boy, you crazy. Old Man Badeau? He'll have us pissin' blood just for lookin' at him. Besides, don't you know what's been goin' on with Tommy J? They be lookin' for a black man. No doubt that bewitched man be number one on their list."

I stepped in between them. "That ain't so, Cully. He ain't bewitched." I said. "Josh and me was sittin' with him just yesterday."

That comment wrinkled Cully's face right up. "Liar." He gave me a shove. "You jist sayin' that to—"

"Why? Why would I make up somethin' like that?" I pointed my thumb at Josh. "Me and Josh had it out last night, and he went runnin' off. Next I know, I catch him sittin' in the rain down the Stink Bug Trail jawin' with Old Man Badeau like he were kin."

Cully turned to Josh and looked him over like he ain't never met the boy before. "Shoulda knew a skinny little orphan would be a kin to a Negro—a bewitched Negro at that."

"Cully," I said, "he ain't no Negro kin and he ain't no orphan. Josh is my brother."

"He ain't no brother. You can't unorphan once you an orphan. He just pretendin' 'til he be gettin' another offer down the road. Heck, the only reason you like him is so you got someone to boss around since your momma's all dried up!"

Cully barely got out that last insult by the time my fist came swinging around at him. But he ducked and swung back.

74

Next thing I knew, we'd grabbed each other and rolled to the ground. We were hitting each other's heads on one of the legs of Cully's bed when Jeannie broke us up.

"Git a hold of yourselves!" she yelled. "What'sa matta' with y'all?"

Cully and I stumbled to our feet and wobbled around.

Cully spoke first. "This…this idget attack me for no reason."

"After you bad-mouthin' my momma."

Jeannie said, "I could care diddly about the fight. I jist don't want that old hag hastlin' us."

Cully and I kept staring at each other, both breathing like we'd just run clear down to Reed's groves and back.

We didn't even notice that Josh was gone until Jeannie asked, "Where that skinny boy?"

I scanned back and forth until I noticed Cully's bedroom window wide open with an army helmet propping it up.

"He dun run off!" cried Cully. I hopped over to the window and Cully said, "You ain't gonna—"

"What?" I said, turning back to Cully. "Ain't you comin'?"

Cully shot a glance at Jeannie and then pushed me out of the way. "Me first," he said and jimmied his way out. I jumped out and before I could stand, Jeannie was practically landing on top of me.

"Shoot, girl," I said.

"Well, you weren't thinkin' you leavin' me behind, were ya?"

"Quit your jawin'!" Cully barked. "Let's find that boy before Old Man Badeau got him in a stew!"

*   *   *

We were on a roundabout course headin' to the Stink Bug Trail when we were stopped in our tracks by a line of men and police cars. There were about twenty cops, some in uniform and some in brown or blue denim. The ones not in uniform wore badges dangling lopsided from their shirts. Some had dogs and some leaned on their cars like they were waiting on fireworks. Cully, Jeannie, and I hit the ground behind an old rotten log just outside the Peterson farm. The cops were ahead of us, across a field, and to our backs was the farm; a crooked barbed-wired fence separated us from a gang of neehin' goats that bounced around, checking us out.

"Oh, dookie," Cully gulped. "They got guns."

I shushed him.

"You kiddin' me? They fixin' to shoot us dead and you tryin' to shush me?"

This seemed all backwards. Usually it was me talkin' crazy and Cully acting like it weren't no thing. But I couldn't think about being worried. I had to find where Josh had run off to.

"There's Daddy!" Jeannie cried.

Cully and I looked where Jeannie was pointing and sure enough, there stood the frowning giant. He had one of them badges dangling from his shirt like the rest of the men.

"I'm splittin'," Cully decided.

I pulled him back down. "We gotta find Josh."

"That boy can get shot up without me."

"What about Old Man Badeau?"

"He's so buddy-buddy with the Negro, some of that black magic might serve him good. Besides, he just some crumby orphan anyhow."

I hit him in the arm. "That's my brother you bad-mouthin'."

"Ain't you two ever stop?" Jeannie busted in. "Them police fixin' to come our way, and Daddy'll smash all our heads in if he spot us." She pointed a thumb and we both looked.

A head man barked out orders to the rest. He pointed at a group of cops and then toward a line of trees; then he pointed at another group and a different line of trees. I was about to say something when the leader pointed straight toward us.

"Oh, cheese and crackers!" Cully cursed. "They gonna git us!"

"C'mon!" I ordered in a loud whisper. I dove under the barbed-wire fence behind us. Cully and Jeannie followed. Partway through, a pair of goats made a fuss and kicked at my head. "Git! Git!" I swatted, and they jumped back.

After freeing myself, I heard Jeannie whining and I pulled up on the wire. "C'mon!" I whispered. "Get that butt wigglin'!"

She got through and started up on her feet, but I yanked her back down.

"Keep low." I searched the area ahead. Just in front of us was a lopsided stack of hay. I jumped behind it. Cully and Jeannie joined me. When I landed, the ground felt all sorts of soft and smelly.

"What the…" Cully said, noticing it himself.

"Git off me!" Jeannie swatted at a pair of goats dancing next to her. She turned to me. "Now what? We lying in goat poo!"

Cully and I shushed her just as the police reached the fence. The goats went crazy, and the dogs barked and yanked them cops along. "Down, boy! Down!" yelled one of the police. "You scaring the bejesus out of them goats."

The goats kept neehin' and hoppin' around so much, they nearly knocked over the hay that hid us. Couple of them stomped their sharp hooves right into my back and I about yelped. I slapped my hand to my face, accidentally scooping a heap of goat dung into my mouth. I gagged, coughing and spitting.

"Ooo-eee!" One of the cops said. "Them goats must be sicker than a mess of rats, all that coughin'."

"Keep your focus, Jenkins," said another with a deeper gruff to his voice. "We ain't lookin' for sick goats."

77

"How we get over the fence, Lieutenant?"

"How should I know?"

"Can't we just go around?"

"We ain't goin' around. That old coot could be anywheres, Jenkins. We gotta get up into that barn up'n there."

"How 'bout if just ask at the farm house to let us in?"

"Hey! I'm in charge here, Jenkins," the gruff voice answered. Then after a pause, "Head on up and ask at the farm house. We'll take the dogs up and 'round the way."

We could hear the barking dogs get further and further away.

"C'mon," Cully said to me. "Let's head on over to the barn."

"You kiddin'? They just said they was headin' that way."

"But we out in the open here, numskull!"

Jeannie spoke up. "I wanna head back home."

I pointed toward a tree line. "We can't head back there. It's crawling with police."

"What's it matter?" Cully snapped. "There're police every which way. Fine mess you got us in, No Good!"

"This was just as much your doin'."

"Well, we can't just walk right up to them police," said Cully. "Us all covered in goat dung. They'd shoot our heads off the second we popped 'em up."

I peeked over the hay. "We could try goin' over to that patch of woods. I don't see no police over there yet."

"Hey, git your head down," said Cully.

Jeannie crept up next to me and asked, "And how we gonna get there without getting caught?"

"Well...real quiet like, I gue—"

"What's going on?" Cully said

I smiled. "I got an idea."

Cully turned his head to where I was lookin'. "What is it?"

I dove over the hay and squirmed toward a pair of goats. They jumped and hopped away from me, but I reached out and snagged the leg of one of them. It kicked. I jumped up and tackled the goat and it went crazy, kickin' and screamin'.

"Wha...you crazy, No Good?" Cully called out in a loud whisper. "They gonna hear!"

I ignored Cully and went right on with my plan. I dragged the squirming goat across the ground all the way to the fence. Then I grabbed a dangling barbed wire and wrapped it around and around the goat's horns 'til it was good and tight. Then I let go. The goat tried to run off, but the other end of that barbed wire was still stuck to the fence, so the goat was stuck.

I turned back to the hay. "C'mon!"

I got up and started hightailing it to the barn, which was also toward that patch of woods I had spotted earlier. I jumped inside the open door, followed a few seconds later by Cully and Jeannie.

Cully was shaking his head as he tried to catch his breath. "You...you crazy, No Good!"

Outside the barn, we could hear that poor goat screamin' and kickin' around. In no time, dogs were barking and the police were running on over.

"Ah...it's just a dumb old goat stuck on the fence," said one of the cops. "C'mon. Help me free him."

I waved toward the barn's backdoor. "C'mon. While they busy."

We headed on out the back door and ran to the far end of the farm to a low rusted metal gate. I jumped over with one push off the top; Cully followed. But Jeannie got stuck halfway.

"Help!" she said in a loud whisper. We tugged her over, but her shorts tore as she hit the ground. "Ah!"

"Hey! You kids!" I looked up and one of the police near the stuck goat was pointing right at us, waving his rifle in the air. "Hold up!"

"Let's go!" Cully said. He shot off into the woods.

I helped Jeannie to her feet and we ran.

We jumped and bounced from tree to tree, all the while hearing those dogs barking away. My heart pounded so hard it felt like it was good and ready to pop. I didn't dare look around; I kept my eyes forward so I didn't bust my head on a branch.

Cully looked back at us and it wasn't two seconds before he smacked his face against the side of a tree. "Ugh!"

I about stepped on him. I yanked him to his feet but he slipped back down again. I looked back to Jeannie; she was running as fast as she could with one hand holding up her torn pants. She was cursing up a storm with every step. I couldn't see the police behind us but I could hear them just fine. With all the cracking and snapping of branches, they sounded like a pack of buffalo chargin' through the woods.

Cully stumbled to his feet again. "C'mon!" I yelled, and Cully and I took off.

Those dogs kept barking and those branches kept snapping.

I jumped over a fallen tree and tumbled right into a creek.

SPLASH!

I smacked face-first into the water. I came up coughing and choking just in time for Jeannie to land right on top of me. I came out of the water again and slipped on the soft, slick creek bottom. Cully was standing on a tree that spanned the creek.

"Stop playin' in the water!"

I stood and the creek came up to my waist. Jeannie and I climbed up the steep other side of the creek bank. Cully stood at the top next to a bald cypress, which had huge roots that fanned out from the trunk a few feet from the ground. The base of the tree looked like a poofy wooden Indian teepee.

"C'mon!" Cully urged us toward him.

We followed him down between a split of roots that took us to the tiny cave under the cypress. Cully grabbed a bunch of fallen branches and rammed them up into the split where we had entered the cave. Now the only light came from the small gaps between the roots. From this hiding spot, we could peek out between them.

We peered out over the creek.

The dogs were barking up a storm. I held my breath when I saw the branches and bushes across the creek shaking. A bald, mean-looking police popped his head up over a bush and looked directly at us. I leaned away from the crack, hoping he hadn't see our eyes between the cypress roots. I looked at Cully and Jeannie. They were watching every move that police made. I leaned forward again, and the police was still peering over a bush. I could see the head of the dog he had on a leash. The dog jumped up and down like a little brother trying to sneak a peek.

Another police called out from somewhere down the creek. I couldn't outright understand his words, but he sounded all sorts of excited, like he'd found something. The bald police took off down the creek, leaving us there with nothing else to look at. All we could do was just sit there scared and shivering and imagine what was going on.

The sounds of the police grew more and more distant and echoing, but no doubt they were excited about something. The dogs kept barking and the cops kept yelling. But then all at once the commotion died down. All that was left was a dog yelpin' on occasion.

"They caught someone," Cully summed up.

"How you knowin' that?" Jeannie whispered back.

"I got ears, don't I? They caught someone, no doubt."

"Think it's Old Man Badeau?" I asked.

Cully turned to me. "Or that orphan."

I was gonna tell Cully off for callin' Josh an orphan again, but I was too nervous to be fighting 'bout that.

81

"How long we gotta be in here?" asked Jeannie.

"'Til they leave us alone," Cully said.

"How long will that be?"

"How should I know? Now, quit your naggin' before you git us all caught."

We got quiet after that. It took a good ten minutes before them police and dogs walked off far enough that we couldn't hear them no more. All the while, we smacked ants and other invisible bugs that crawled up our legs, arms, face, and neck.

Cully'd had enough. He pushed off the branches covering our exit and jumped out. Jeannie and I followed.

"Shoot, man!" he cursed as he danced around just outside the tree. "They bitin' me like a—"

"Hey!"

"Ah! What the dobby?" Cully jumped.

We looked up and there was Jacob and Seth standing in between a pair of trees wearing their typical cow-faced expressions.

"Warn us next time you go sneakin' up," said Cully. "How'd you get past them police, anyhow?"

Jacob stepped forward. "We were just mindin' our own business when we hear'ed them dogs a-barkin'. So we scooted on up a tree and watched them all scurrying around like they out to kill."

"Yeah," Seth said. "What'd y'all do?"

"What you mean?" Cully said, still flicking a few bugs off his legs. "Ain't you heard about Tommy J?"

"What'd he do?"

"What'd he do? Man. Where you been?" Cully spat. "He's been murdered dead and them police be huntin' down the killer."

Seth turned to his brother. "That's why he was a-runnin'."

"He who?" I asked. "What'd you seen?"

Jacob looked at Seth and then at me. "Old Man Badeau, that's who. We saw him runnin' off like a crazy man with them police right behind him."

"They catch him?"

"No. But they almost did. That orphan was slowin' him up."

"Josh?" I said. "You saw Josh?"

"Yeah. He was runnin' side by side with Old Man Badeau. Except when he fall and that Negro had to stop and pick him back up."

"Serves him right," Cully said.

I turned to Cully. "What d'ya mean by that?"

"You know that Negro got that boy under his black magic. Probably gonna eat him up when the time come right."

"He ain't got no black magic. He just an old Negro."

"If it whatn't for that stupid orphan runnin' off, we wouldn't be here in the first place. Got me all bit up. Lost in these ninnyhammer woods."

"I thought you knew where we was," Jeannie said.

"I know where we is! Just up outside the Peterson farm. Point is, I thought we was hittin' the Stink Bug Trail and headin' home. In fact, that's just where I'm headin' to now. Home. Better leave now before them police come and shoot us dead." Cully started off, then stopped. "Ain't y'all comin'?"

Jeannie looked at me. "I ain't goin' home without Josh," I said.

"You crazy. I'm goin' home. C'mon, Jeannie."

Jeannie shook her head. "I'm stayin'. No Good gonna need help findin' that boy."

Cully put his hands on his hips and tilted his head. "Help? Jeannie, you 'bout as useless as tits on a bull."

Jeannie crossed her arms and snarled at her little brother.

Cully shook his head again. "I'm leavin'." He looked at Jacob and Seth. "You comin'?"

The brothers looked at each other.

"Which way they chase Josh out?" I asked them.

Jacob spun his head around and pointed. "Up that way apiece."

Cully walked past them, and without anyone sayin' another word, Jacob and Seth followed him out. They crossed the creek at the fallen tree and disappeared into the woods.

I turned to Jeannie. "Thanks," I said.

She smiled.

"Okay." I took a deep breath. "Let's head on out."

Nine

Soaked

Before long, it was midday, and the woods were getting downright musty with the baking sun burning the swamp moss off the trees. Our clothes were still wet and nasty from falling in the creek hours before. Yet for every drop of blackwater that dried from our clothes, a drop of sweat took its place. And to top it off, my stomach was growlin' like an angry cat.

We came to another creek, and I stopped off to take a drink. Jeannie crouched down next to me but she slipped on a rock and landed on her butt.

"Ow!"

"Watch out, Jeannie."

She stood up. "I can't help it. These stupid pants been slippin' down ever since I tore them on that stupid goat fence."

I checked out her shorts. They were ripped on the side and she had tied a knot along the waist to tighten them, but they was drooping down anyhow.

"I'll fix 'em up."

I stepped over to some crab grass that was growing along the creek and snapped off a grassy runner. I walked over to Jeannie and wrapped the runner around her waist like a belt; I strung it through a couple loops in her shorts and tied it off. "There ya go."

I looked up at Jeannie, and she was giving me this expression that made me all sorts of uneasy.

"What you smirkin' at?" I took a step back.

"Oh, nothin'." She dropped her chin and kept right on lookin' at me, twiddling a curly piece of hair that dangled over her ear. "You know, you kinda cute when you and Cully ain't goin' at it."

I turned and took a few steps away. "I ain't cute."

"Yes you is. You just don't know it."

"I should know whether I'm cute or not, and I ain't."

Jeannie giggled.

I shook my head. "Ah…I'm hungry." I stepped up to a good climbing oak and worked my way up.

"Whatcha doin'?" Jeannie asked.

I pulled myself up to a branch and peered out over the treetops. In one direction, I could see the scattered buildings of downtown Sanford off in the distance, and in the other nothing but woods. "Lookin' for a break in the trees."

"How come?" she called out from the base of the oak.

"Don't you know nothin'? I'm lookin' for a celery farm!"

"What? You see somethin'?"

"No. There ain't spit out there. We lost somethin' good."

"You see what kind of wood?"

"Not wood! Good! We lost somethin' good! I…uh…wha…"

"What? What you see?"

Up ahead, I saw some wrestling going on in a tree. I tried to decide if it was a person or some kind of animal. It was

86

shaking too much for a squirrel or a bird, and I hoped it wasn't no black bear.

"No Good! What d'you see?"

"Pipe down, will ya! I see somethin', but..." I saw a head pop up over some branches. The face smiled at me and the boy waved his hand in the air. "Well, I'll be," I said.

I shimmied down the tree and shot through the bushes toward the commotion. Jeannie tried to keep up.

"What? What'd you see?"

When I reached the tree, I looked up and there was Ansel, sitting as proud as a puppy with a bone. He scooted down and plopped down in front of us. Ansel was about three-quarters my size, stringy hair and scrapes up and down his arms and legs from all the tree climbin'. He had on a button-down shirt with no buttons, showing his bony chest. He had on baggy shorts that were almost falling off his hips, and on his feet were what used to be nice Sunday church shoes with no socks.

"Ah, man," said Jeannie. "It's just Ansel. Thought it was Josh."

"We huntin' for Josh, my brother," I explained to Ansel. "Jacob and Seth said he was runnin' off from the cops with—"

Ansel got an excited look in his eyes and started pointing behind him.

"You saw them?"

He nodded and smiled. It occurred to me that Ansel had the most beautiful teeth I had ever seen—all white, straight, and full. Since the boy never talked, I'd never previously had the occasion to check them out.

I pointed ahead. "Lead the way."

Ansel took off down the trail so fast I could barely keep up. He was hopping logs and zipping through scrubby fronds like there was candy waitin' for him.

Jeannie let the cursing fly. "Ansel! Slow it down!"

Ansel would stop to allow me to catch my breath and Jeannie to catch up, but then he'd shoot off again. The boy had only two speeds: stop and go.

Ansel jumped over one bush and hopped onto a fallen tree that crossed a fast-moving creek. I jumped over the bush, slipped on the slick tree, and slammed right into his back. "Oh, sh—" I started to say as Ansel bounced off me and fell, smacking his head hard on a rock stickin' out of the creek. His body rolled and slipped into the rushing water. The current swept him downriver.

"Ansel!" I called out, but the boy was out cold, floating away with only his back breaking the surface. "Criminelly!" I said, and I jumped right in after him.

I hit the water and the current dragged at me good and hard.

I heard Jeannie scream. "No Good!"

I kept swimming forward, zigzagging to avoid the rocks and branches and swollen tree trunks. My arms and legs scraped past a thorny branch, and then a rock, and then another rock. "An...Ansel!" I gurgled. I was bouncing around so much, I couldn't see nothin' ahead of me but water splashing up into my face.

Before I could steady myself, I felt a tug on the back of shirt and I was lifted straight out of the water. Before I could even spit, I hit the muddy ground. I looked up and saw none other than Old Man Badeau starin' down on me.

His deep voice bellowed, "You kids ain't nothin' but trouble."

I spit out some of the blackwater, wiped my eyes, and turned. Next to Old Man Badeau was Ansel who looked asleep, with a kid kneeling over him. It took me a minute to realize that the kid was Josh.

Josh turned to me and smiled.

I smiled back. "Josh! Shoot, boy, where you been?"

"Watch your language, boy," said Old Man Badeau.

88

"What you care? You're jus—" I stopped myself.

"What? I'm what?" The old man shook his head, placing his giant hands on his hips. "Boy, to you I may be some old Negro livin' out in the woods. But I jist saved your life. Sometimes you gotta look past what you've been taught and realize that you talkin' to someone not two steps away from your kin."

I stared at him, head tilted. I must've looked like an old dog tryin' to read Shakespeare.

Old Man Badeau turned to Josh and then to Ansel.

I realized Ansel was missing his shorts. "He ain't got no pants on."

"They slip'd off when I yanked him outta th'creek," said Old Man Badeau. "No bother. We best get that boy to a doctor."

"He bleedin' from the ear," said Josh.

Old Man Badeau nodded. "I'll carry him." He bent down and tossed Ansel over his giant shoulder like bag of corn. Josh stepped up next to him.

The old man turned to me. "You two comin'?"

I looked over my shoulder and there was Jeannie, peeking out from behind a tree. I realized right away that she was probably trying to hide from the old man.

Old Man Badeau took off walking.

I stood up and nearly fell over, my legs all jelly-like.

"You okay?" Josh asked.

"I'm fine. I'm fine." I turned back to Jeannie. "Just stay next to me and Josh." I nodded to the old man who was a couple trees away by now. "He's scary, but he's all right."

*   *   *

It was like that old Negro had a compass in his head, 'cause he had us on the outskirts of downtown Sanford in no time. Sneaking down a back alley, he led us into an abandoned building that had no roof and was missing half its bricks. He had to duck his head to step through a hole in one of the walls.

Old Man Badeau set Ansel down on the dirty cement floor next to a pile of rags. He stepped over to a stack of wooden crates and sat on one. It creaked. He pointed to the pile. "Find that boy a change of clothes."

Josh immediately walked over and started digging.

"You mean for Ansel?" I objected. "Them's just rags."

"He as cold as fish now and liable to catch his death. They ain't fancy, but they'll work in a pinch."

My head spun back and forth between the rags and Old Man Badeau. I looked at Jeannie, but she was just standing there staring at Ansel and his wet skivvies hanging out for all the world to see. I turned to Josh, who was now strugglin' to yank off Ansel's wet shirt.

"You crazy, Josh? Why you strippin' Ansel with a girl here watchin'? Besides, he needs a doctor. Why we wasting time here?"

Old Man Badeau shook his head. "You forever shootin' off your mouth. In case you ain't realizin', there's a hunt goin' on 'round town and they ain't lookin' for no white man. They lookin' for a Negro like me. Now if I was to go stompin' into a hospital with a white boy all beat up and unclothed, they wouldn't wait a rooster's doodle-do before they slap me in jail or worse. I'd like to see you all off and safe, but this is where we part. I gotta head on out 'til this ruckus is all died down. Meanwhile, you'ins gotta fetch a doc over here. Lessen you gonna carry that boy the rest of the way."

I stood there numbed with everything Old Man Badeau had rattled off.

From behind, Josh said, "When we seein' you again?"

Old Man Badeau smiled. "Don't you worry 'bout that."

Old Man Badeau's knees popped when he stood, then he floated out of the hole we entered like a ghost.

I turned to Jeannie and Josh, not sure what to do. Josh finished yanking off Ansel's shirt. His naked body was pale and wet. He was still out cold, but I could see in his chest he was shivering.

Jeannie bent down to the rags and fished out dirty, ripped overalls. "Push him up and I'll slip these on him," she told Josh.

"Well...well..." I stuttered. "I guess I'll find the doctor."

Jeannie and Josh didn't say a word.

"I'll be back," I said and headed out.

*   *   *

A gush of iodine-stenched air hit me like a bee sting to the face. I gave my nose a pinch as I made my way into the entrance of Sanford Central Hospital. Noisy, rattling fans lined two of the walls, whipping up a chilling breeze for my damp clothes.

"Boy! Hey, you! Boy!"

A homely young nurse shuffled up to me, looking like she was fixin' to swat a cockroach.

"This is no place to play. Run along. Run along."

She gripped my shoulders and spun me back toward the door. My shoes squeaked across the tiled floor.

"Wait! Hold on!" I wiggled out of her grip and faced her again. "My friend. He needs a doctor."

"Your friend?" She let out a huff. "Your imaginary friend—I've heard all the jokes. Now run along and don't come back unless you're with an adult."

She stretched out her arm to push me along, but I jerked away. "Honest. He's in that broken building a couple blocks up the street. He bleedin' from the ear."

"The doctors don't make house calls. Tell your friend to—"

"I can't. He out like the dead."

91

"Dead? Boy. Death is nothing to joke about. Now, get out!"

I twisted away from her and nearly slammed into a second nurse, this one taller and much older.

"What's going on here?" asked the older nurse, her voice harsh and crackly.

"This boy is causing trouble."

"I am not! I came in 'cause my friend Ansel slipped into the creek and got walloped on his head and now he bleedin' out his ear and this nurse ain't doin' diddly to fetch him a doctor before he stone dead."

The old nurse took a step toward me, and I stepped back. She glared me down like God himself. "You shall speak to my nurses with more respect, young man."

I swallowed.

But then she said, "Where's your friend?"

"Down the road apiece."

The old nurse looked at the younger one and said, "Get Doctor Hammond."

"But he's with—"

"Just tell them Nurse Braddock wants him out in the lobby now. He'll come."

*   *   *

I don't know how I did it. Somehow I fell asleep lying across a row of squeaky wooden chairs in the hospital lobby. I didn't wake up until Josh jabbed me five or six times with his bony fingers. I rolled off and smacked my head on the cold tiled floor.

"Shoot, Josh." I sat up, rubbing my head. "Why'd you—"

I stopped at the sight of Pa glaring down at me, fired up and ready to pop.

I jumped to my feet. "Uh…hi, uh…Pa."

"Don't you hi me, boy."

I could tell in his voice that he was madder than a bulldog on a chain at a squirrel circus. This scared me something fierce. Pa almost never lost his cool.

"Now, I recall telling you and Josh to stay at Cully's, or was I mistaken?"

"No, Pa. That's what you said."

"Then how come I'm finding you two at the hospital of all places? Don't you realize what's going on out there? Don't you realize how lucky you two are that you didn't get your butts blown off?"

"Yes, sir."

"No Good, I just don't know what to do with you sometimes. It's like you got a hole in your skull."

I dropped my head.

"Na, you don't. Look at me when I'm speakin'."

I looked up.

"Now, I don't ever want to catch you running off like you did when something like this happens. It'd break your Momma's heart if I had to tell her that her son done got himself killed 'cause he thought chasing a little danger would be more fun than listenin' to his old man." He jammed his finger into my chest. "You hearin' me?"

"I'm hearin' you, Pa."

He stared at me good and hard. For the silent seconds that followed, I shook so hard inside that tears started workin' their way out.

"Pa?"

"What?"

"Ansel gonna make it?"

Pa smiled unexpectedly. He nodded slowly. "Yeah. He fine. Just a bump on the head. His momma in with him now."

I gave a good swipe of my nose with my arm and breathed in the snot left over.

"Now…" Pa said, slowly mounting each of his hands on his hips. "You go and take Josh back home. Momma's already workin' herself sick over you two."

I turned to Josh. He looked just as scared as I felt.

"And drop Jeannie home along the way."

I turned to my other side, and there was Jeannie leaning against the wall looking back at us.

I turned back to Pa. "You mean alone? What about…"

"Just head straight on home. And I mean straight home. You'll be alright." He reached into his pocket and pulled out some coins. "Here's some money for the bus."

I let him drop the coins in my hand and I stared at it like it was gold. I could count on one hand how many times I had ever held money, and this was the first time Pa had ever just handed me some out of the blue.

I took a step toward the door.

Then Pa added, "We done caught Tommy J's Negro killer anyhow."

I stopped. Eyes wide, I looked up at Pa. "You caught 'im? Who dun it?"

Pa shook his head. "Don't you no never mind. He in jail. Just git!"

Josh, Jeannie, and I shot out the door. We jumped across the street just as the bus was slowing down. Climbing up the bus steps, I held up a couple of Pa's coins to the fare box, but it had a sign on it that read Broken. The driver pointed his foot to a wicker basket next to him and I dropped the coins in. We claimed a few seats.

A pair of kids in new slacks and collared shirts stared at us like we were dirt. I shifted in my seat, trying to ignore them.

The bus barely pulled out when Josh tugged on my shirt. "You don't think they caught…"

"Old Man Badeau?" I whispered. My eyes shot at the nearby kids and I feared they heard me.

I looked to Josh. He nodded.

I said, "Jist what I was thinkin'."

Josh paused. "I guess we ain't goin' straight home."

"Oh, no," Jeannie said. "Ain't we had enough for one day?"

I smiled at Josh and Jeannie. "It won't take but a couple minutes. Besides, Jeannie. No one making you tag along. You can head on home."

Jeannie looked out the window and down the road.

"Well?" I asked.

"Well, nothin'!" Jeannie snapped. "You two can't be trusted runnin' off alone. Where we headin'?"

Josh gave a weak smile.

Ten

Imprisoned

When Jeannie, Josh, and I stepped off the bus, the stink from the town dump nearly caused me to fall over. The bus rattled and kicked up some dust as it took off down the road. We followed an even dustier dirt road toward the stink. The evening sun was shining dead in our faces, and the mosquitoes were biting. I turned away from the sun and could hear Jeannie and Josh slapping off the bugs.

"You sure the jail's this way?" Jeannie asked.

I spun around and walked backwards. "Course I'm sure."

"Woo! God, that stinks!" she said.

Josh looked at me. I read the question on his face and thumbed toward the side. "The town dump. All sorts of garbage been rottin' here for the past hundred years."

We all faced where I was thumbing. The dirt road we were walking on was empty and endless with trees lining both sides. Up ahead were huge mounds taller than the tallest tree.

Although they were a good half-mile or so ahead of us, the smell was so bad, it was like we were standing on top of them.

"Woo!" Jeannie went on. "I can't barely stand it. It smell like wet cocky."

I ignored Jeannie and focused on Josh. His face wore a serious, anxious expression. "Hey, Josh. Don't worry. We'll head back home soon. Pa gave me enough money that we can take the bus again." I rattled the coins around in my pocket.

"It ain't that," he said.

"Then what?" I stopped and touched Josh's chest. He stopped and looked up at me. "You frettin' over Old Man Badeau, ain't cha, Josh?" I said. "I knew I shoulda told you this a while back, but it ain't healthy takin' a liking to a Negro. And I ain't talkin' about Cully's mumbo jumbo stuff and him having black magic. I'm just sayin', Negros like him ain't nothin' but trouble. Why you think he livin' like a bum out in the woods? No one will take 'im, that's why."

"He ain't all bad," Josh said weakly.

"I ain't sayin' that neither. Heck, if it weren't for him, Ansel would be belly-up in that creek."

"So would you," Jeannie added.

"I woulda been fine. My point is, he ain't bad. He just trouble. And you ain't never gotta look for trouble. Trouble'll find you all by itself."

"Then why we goin' to some stupid jail?" Jeannie huffed.

I turned to her. "Jeannie. You as bad as Josh with all the questions." Then I explained to her like she was slow in the head, "We goin' just to make sure he ain't there. Tommy J can't get the scoop no more, can he? Sometimes, Jeannie, you as clueless as an oik."

Jeannie's face crunched and she fired her fist straight into my belly. I toppled over, and my butt hit the dirt road.

"Why'd you do that for?" I yelled, catching my breath.

Jeannie kept right on walking. "No reason."

I looked at Josh. "What you smirkin' at?"

97

Josh tried to unsmile and caught up with Jeannie.

I stood and rubbed my stomach for a couple more seconds before I called out, "Hold up. I'm comin'."

*   *   *

The jail was also about a half-mile down the road. Flocks of seagulls were yellin' out their "Hack-kack-kack!" as they dived and dipped around the trash mounds across the street. Sometimes they picked off bits of trash in their beaks, swooped toward the jail, and then fought each other, causing some of the trash to sprinkle down on us.

"Stupid birds!" Jeannie cursed, brushing off a blackened orange peel from her shoulder.

"Shhhh!" I said as I pressed my back against an old wooden shed just outside a rusting chain-link fence. The fence surrounded a concrete building that looked like a beat-up hotel out of a cowboy movie, but with bars instead of windows.

Jeannie pressed in against the shed wall next to me. "How you even know about this place?"

"I helped my Uncle Travis take some trash to the dump a while back, and he told me all about it. Said it used to be a house of bear-lesk until the cops made it a jail for Negros."

"Bear-lesk?" Josh asked.

"Uncle Carl said it was like a full-service hotel," I explained. "First class, I'd reckon."

"How come they built a hotel next to the dump?" Jeannie asked.

I shrugged. "Guess that's why it's a jail now."

"What we do now?" asked Josh.

"Yeah, No Good! You dragged us here," said Jeannie. "How you thinkin' we gonna get in there?"

"We ain't goin' in there. What, you think they gonna let a few kids just walk right into a Negro jail? You crazy."

"Then why we here, No Good?"

"They gonna bring the prisoners out. It was this time when Uncle Carl and I came out here and them Negros were all hangin' out in that yard beside the jail." I pointed to the empty area of white-sand gravel outside the jail and surrounded by the fence. "Uncle Carl said they take them out once a day so they don't go all crazy inside."

"Oh, really?" Jeannie said. "Then where they at? The only ones outside is us and those stupid birds!"

"Shhhh!" I said as a door on the side of the jail let out a heavy clank and screeched long and loud like a cat on a wringer.

Jeannie, Josh, and I pressed against each other to see around the edge of the shed. Two huge cops waddled out of a barred door, lookin' bored and mean. Behind them was a line of Negros, all with chains on their hands and feet. They created a constant rattlin' sound that got louder and louder the more Negros that came. I kept my eyes on their faces. They were all big and dressed in faded blue jumpsuits, so it was hard to tell them apart. A couple times, I glanced at Josh quick to see if he recognized Old Man Badeau. He kept the same wide-eyed stare.

The last Negro stepped out and another cop followed behind. I looked over every Negro face. Not one of them was Old Man Badeau. I looked over at Josh again and this time he looked back. For once, he appeared relieved.

CLANK-THUD!

I turned back to the jail. From the door had come one last Negro, now lying face-down on the chalk-white ground. A cop stood in the doorway behind him, laughing. The Negro lifted his head. His face was as bloody as a hamburger before it's cooked.

"Old Man Badeau…" whispered Jeannie.

For the first time since I'd known him, the strong old man looked weak. And with his swollen eyes, he seemed almost asleep.

"Git up!" the laughing cop yelled, and he gave him a big ol' kick in the pants.

Old Man Badeau rolled himself up to his knees and did some coughing. The cop kicked him again, and Old Man Badeau fell to the ground again.

"No!" I heard Josh yelp.

I looked down and Josh was bitin' one of his fingers like he was watchin' a horror picture.

"Git up," the cop ordered.

The old Negro struggled up, slow and weak. He made it to his feet but kept his head down.

The cop laughed again just as a group of seagulls fightin' over some trash called out, "Hack-kack-kack!"—as though they were laughing along with the cop. I don't know why, but I suddenly felt like grabbing a slingshot and knockin' them dumb old birds down.

The cops grouped up together, slapped each other on the backs and sassed each other 'bout something I didn't follow. Old Man Badeau and the rest of the Negros were left alone.

None spoke a word. They just wandered around the open area, heads down and shufflin' their feet like pouting children. Old Man Badeau moved slower than the rest. He eventually made it to the fence nearest to us, but he paid no never mind to the shed we hid behind; he just leaned the side of his head against the fence and breathed with a wheezing sound.

Old Man Badeau was so close, I wanted to call out to him and get his attention. But my mouth was stone dry and my head hadn't a thought in it.

Before I could move or speak a word, Josh shot out and ran to the fence.

"Josh…" I whispered, but he was already gone.

Josh slid along the ground on his knees just opposite Old Man Badeau. He grabbed a couple links in the fence and stuck a few fingers through. I couldn't see the look on Old Man Badeau's face from the shed, but I could see him lift his head.

"That boy's crazy," whispered Jeannie.

My eyes shot over to the cops. They were still laughin' and jawin' away at each other. Old Man Badeau stood between them and Josh. The boy was so paper thin and Old Man Badeau so big, I figured they couldn't see Josh even if they were watching.

I could hear the low grumble of Old Man Badeau's voice, but couldn't tell what he was sayin' to Josh.

"He gonna get us caught," Jeannie said.

I wanted to say somethin', but my mouth and head were as empty as ever. And by the time I looked at Josh again, he was boltin' back to the shed.

Standing next to me, I could feel Josh's body shivering like he was cold. I saw that his face was wet with tears. I shook my head at him and looked up at Old Man Badeau. The big man was shufflin' away from the fence.

I whispered to Josh and Jeannie, "We best catch the bus."

Eleven

The Bombshell

It was dark by the time we got to Cully's house.

"Good night, No Good. Josh." Jeannie gave Josh and me a lazy wave as she swaggered up her porch.

The locusts were out and chirpin' away, and Josh and I hadn't said word one to each other. It wasn't until my foot hit the first step of the porch that I noticed Pa standing at the front door starin' down at us like a hungry mountain lion.

I stopped and looked up at him, Josh next to me.

"Trouble with the bus?" his deep voice grumbled.

I stuttered, "Uh…we…we was…"

The porch squeaked as he stepped forward. "You ain't gotta search for no lie, No Good. I knew where you was."

I frowned.

"Didn't you wonder why I gave you all that change for the bus? Or ain't you that inquisitive?"

"Well…yeah."

Pa nodded slow and serious. "You weren't gonna sit still 'til you knew. And now that you gotten that out of your system, I don't want you ever goin' down there again. Understood?"

"Yes, sir."

"You too, Josh. I know No Good drags you along. But you gotta anchor this boy to the ground. Lord knows he needs it."

Josh nodded.

"Okay," Pa summed up, taking his time staring at me and then Josh. "Now get your butts inside. Momma got a wooden spoon with your names on it."

I started to move, when Josh spoke up.

"Dinner?"

I stopped.

Pa nodded. "Yeah. Can't have you two starve to death. Now, git!"

We shot inside. And as Pa promised, we got our backsides whacked and our stomachs filled. I still smelled like creek water from earlier that day, so Momma scrubbed us both raw with the dishrag. And since it was late, she didn't have time to heat up the bathwater, so she went at it cold. It felt like we were scraped with a chunk of ice.

After she was done, she didn't hassle us one word. All she said was, "Okay. Head on to bed."

Can't tell what made me say it, but as I stepped out of the tub and grabbed my towel, I turned and said, "Thanks, Momma."

She didn't say nothin' at first, just gave me her rough mouth smile. Then she said, "Head on to bed."

*   *   *

Josh and I lay in bed, me feelin' beaten up and chilly. But the bed felt so good, it all just went away like the dew.

"Josh?" I whispered. My bedroom door was closed and Momma and Pa were still creaking around out in the living room.

"Ya?"

"What'd he say to you? Old Man Badeau, I mean."

Josh didn't say nothin'.

"When you went crazy and ran to him, I heard him talkin', but couldn't make it out. What'd he say?"

Josh paused again, but then said, "He…he just said not to worry."

"Worry? Why we worry? He the one in jail."

"It don't matter."

"What don't matter? Josh, you ain't makin' a spit of sense."

"It don't matter what he said."

"Then why'd you run to him? You coulda got us all caught, you know. I figure you had to hear him say somethin', or you had to say somethin' to him. You say somethin' to him?"

"It don't matter, Johnny."

"It does matter if it means getting caught. Just tell me. What'd you talk about?"

"You wouldn't understand."

I sat up in bed. "What you mean? You sayin' I'm slow? Boy, you best do some talkin' or my fist will fire up that memory." I looked at the bedroom door, realizing how loud I was getting. I could still hear Momma and Pa moving around. I turned to Josh.

Josh looked up at me and then turned on his side, his back to me. I was about to say somethin' else when he dropped the bombshell: "He my grandpappy."

"Say what?"

Josh didn't say nothin'.

I gave him a shove and started talkin' like a nervous beaver. "Josh. What d'you mean he your grandpappy? That don't make no sense. How can an orphan have a Negro pappy? Or any pappy? Wha—"

"Johnny..." Josh said, turning to me. "He my grandpappy. My momma died a while back. And he be watching after me every place I go."

"What...you mean, he treats you like he your grandpappy?"

Josh sat up, his back to the wall. "No, Johnny. He my grandpappy. My real grandpappy. My momma was his daughter."

I peered at Josh, still trying to figure him out. I could barely see his narrow face in the darkness. "How'd...what'd you..."

"You gotta promise not to tell no one. I ain't never told a soul and Grandpappy said if I do, I'll lose him for good. But seeing how he in jail..."

"Tell what? You still ain't makin' no sense. Josh, there ain't no way Old Man— I mean...you know who I mean. There ain't no way... He be a Negro, for Christ sake."

"Johnny..."

Josh turned toward the door. I turned with him. Momma and Pa were still creaking away. By the time I turned back to Josh, he was starin' at me.

"It's like this, Johnny. I don't know my pa. My momma didn't even know him. He one of them white Navy pilots that came and beat up on my momma and next thing she knew it, there I was, as white as sugar. That's what she called me. Her sugar."

Josh turned away again and I waited for him to keep talking.

"I never called her Momma like most kids. I called her Madam. I asked her why other kids get to call their momma Momma, but she just say that we had somethin' special so we had to call each other somethin' special. So I called her Madam. And she called me Sugar. Then one day she got sick. And the sick wouldn't go away. She kept coughing and spittin' up 'til she didn't do nothin' but lay in bed and I had to take care of her. And then one morning I woke up and fixed her some breakfast, but she kept right on sleepin'.'"

Josh stopped talkin' again, and I could hear him suck in some snot. His voice was shaky when he finally started up again.

"When the police came by and asked me where my momma was, and I told them the doctor dun took her away, they…they just didn't believe me. They…they just went right on asking me where my momma was."

Josh was crying good and steady now. But I was frozen solid, like nothin' worked. I just sat there, listening to him sniffle and feeling the bed wiggle. I thought about putting a hand on his shoulder or something a good brother would do. But I couldn't move. It was like my body was there but my brain forgot how it worked.

"I didn't have no one. Until Grandpappy come and found me that night at the shelter. I didn't even know who Madam's daddy was 'til he came by and explain that he hadn't been speakin' with her since she run off after he lost his job at the mill. He didn't even known Madam was sick 'til she was dead and gone. And since they already decided I was an orphan, he couldn't come and take me away neither on account he was Negro. So instead he just followed me around every place I stayed."

I finally found my voice and spoke up. "That's why Old Man… I mean… That's why your…grandpappy…suddenly showed up in Sanford? He was tailin' you?"

Josh nodded. "You wanna know what he said to me at the jail? He told me…he told me that he didn't have to follow me no more. He told me not to worry 'cause I finally had a family."

And that's all Josh had to say. With that, he lay in bed and rolled to his side, his back to me. The bed kept on shaking and I knew he was crying, but I still couldn't touch him. I heard what he said; I just couldn't swallow it. It was like I had an entire orange stuck in my mouth but I forgot how to chew. And the longer I sat there, the harder it became just to breathe.

After some time, I stood up from the bed and stared at Josh's back. The creaking from out in the living room had silenced; Momma and Pa must've turned in for the night. Now my room was as dark as ever.

I rubbed my face good and hard. Dropping my hands, I tried to look at Josh, but all I could see was a dark blur.

Slowly, I reached down, grabbed my pillow, and tossed it on the floor. Lying on the hardwood, my head found the lump of feathers. I closed my eyes and fell asleep.

In all the time I slept in my bedroom, that night was the loneliest of my life.

Twelve

Uncle Travis

I woke up the next morning and Josh was still asleep. I stood and wiggled out my arm, which was feeling all pins and needles after sleeping on the hard floor. I tiptoed past the bed and shot outside to take my morning piss. It wasn't until I walked back inside that my nose and ears finally woke and I smelled and heard snapping sausages cooking on the stove. I ran through the house to the kitchen and slid to a stop.

Without turning from the stove, Momma told me, "Go fetch me some eggs from the icebox."

I jumped to it. "Who we spectin'?" I asked. Pancakes were something special in our house; but sausage and eggs for breakfast was mouse-in-your-drawers crazy. I wouldn't have been surprised if the President of the United States came struttin' through the front door to join us.

I held out the wooden carton of eggs to Momma. She grabbed a couple and placed them on the counter.

I stood there waiting for her to answer.

"Well?" she said. "You waitin' for them eggs to spoil? Stick them back in the icebox."

"Momma…"

She smiled and said, "Uncle Travis."

"Uncle Travis?" I nearly jumped. The eggs bobbled around in the open-ended carton. I jerked to steady them, but one toppled out and smashed on the floor.

"No Good!" Momma yelled. "Put them eggs away!" She bent down with the spatula and dishrag, scooped up as much of the egg as possible, and plopped it down on the skittle next to the sausages.

After I had the eggs back in the icebox, Momma handed me the spatula. "Keep them sausages turnin'," she told me. She bent down and wiped up the remaining dots of egg splatter.

I stepped up to the stove and knocked the links around the sizzling butter and egg. "When will Uncle Travis get here?"

"Any minute," she said from the floor.

"How come you didn't mention it?"

"Well, if you weren't so busy gettin' you and Josh into mischief…"

A loud knock came from the front door.

"Uncle Travis!"

I ran from the kitchen with the spatula still in my hand.

"No Good!" called Momma.

I shot down the hallway to the front door and tossed it open.

The tall, broad-shouldered man gave me a big ol' smile. "Why, it's none other than Mr. Johnny No Good."

"Uncle Travis!" I gave him a hug.

"Hey…hey…hey. Watch it, sport."

I stepped back and he wiped the greasy butter off the side of his khaki army uniform.

"Oh, Travis," Momma said from behind me. "You're gorgeous."

109

"So are you, Emily." He leaned forward and gave her cheek a kiss. "Is that sausage I smell?"

"The food!" Momma yanked the spatula from my hand and took off down the hall.

Uncle Travis picked up the large green duffle bag next to him, threw it over his shoulder, and ruffled my hair with his free hand. "C'mon, sport."

I followed him inside and down the hall like an excited puppy. In the kitchen, he sat at the table in my seat and put his duffle bag next to him.

"That's my chair."

"No Good!" Momma snapped. "Don't be rude. Go'n get yourself a chair from the living room."

I followed Momma's orders and when I got back into the kitchen with the extra chair, Pa was talkin' with Uncle Travis.

"Yeah," Pa went on. "I always said train travel ain't what it used to be. Well, at least you made it here in one piece."

I stuck the chair next to Uncle Travis and sat down. He turned to me and smiled. He was a huge man with bulging muscles that stretched his shirt. I remembered him having curly red hair, but his head was shaved today, with a dark outline of where his hair should be.

"You've grown at least two inches since I last seen you," he told me.

"What'd you bring me?"

"No Good!" Ma yelled, nearly flicking the greasy spatula at me. "Give him a chance to settle in."

Uncle Travis gave his typical smooth, big-faced smile. "Na, it's alright. The boy's just excited, that's all. Besides, I came prepared." He leaned in his duffle bag opposite me and fished through the tight opening. He pulled out his fist and held it out to me, palm down. I could tell he was holding something, but the size of his hand hid it from view.

"What is it?"

He rotated his hand and held out a dirty old baseball.

"A baseball?" I said, disappointed.

"No Good," Pa snapped from the other side of the table, "that ain't no way to talk to your uncle. A gift's a gift. He didn't have to give you nothin'."

Uncle Travis smiled and leaned in to me. "What you don't know is the significance of this ball. You're looking at a baseball that the Ted Williams hit."

"Ted Williams?" I said. "I thought you was in China."

"Japan, sport. I was stationed in Tokyo, Japan."

"You foolin' around with baseball?" Pa said, surprised. "Thought the army was there to rebuild the country, not playin' games."

"Part of our job is to maintain peaceful relations with them Jap-o-nese." He said Jap-o-nese like it was a dirty word. "And let me tell you, them slant-eyed buggers are nuts about baseball. A bunch of us put together a coupla teams to blow off a little steam, and next thing we knew them Japs were joining up and playin' along beside us. They can't hit a ball to save their lives, but they out there every day givin' it a try."

Pa said, "So what's this about Ted Williams?"

"Our company commander saw how we was makin' friends with the Japs, and he pulled some strings and flew none other than Ted Williams all the way out to the base to come by and hit a few balls with us. Let me tell you, the stories are true. That man could hit anything. And he hits it like a dead-eye. He'd point out left field, hit the ball, and the ball would land spot on where he pointed."

"You don't say?" Pa asked. "Well, how 'bout that?"

"And Ted Williams hit this ball?" I said.

"You better believe it."

He tossed the ball to me and I caught it in both hands. I rolled it from hand to hand.

"Wow."

111

Momma spun around with plates filled with sausage and dropped them in front of Pa and Uncle Travis. I took my eyes away from the ball long enough to ogle the sausage. "Eggs a-comin'." Ma said. "Eat up before it goes cold." She dropped another plate in front of me. I reached for a sausage, but Momma slapped my hand.

"But Momma," I said.

"Go wash them hands." I dropped the ball to the table, shot up, and headed toward the hall. "And don't come back without Josh!"

With Uncle Travis and the Ted Williams baseball, I dun forgot about Josh. I jumped into my bedroom and despite all the excitement, Josh was still out like a light. I put my foot on the bed and gave it a few good bounces.

"Git up, Josh."

He groaned and opened his eyes.

"Uncle Travis is here and Momma got sausages on the table."

"Sausages?"

"Git up, or Momma won't let me have none."

I ran out and down the hall to the washroom. I held my breath as I went in and scrubbed my hands good and fast. The washroom's toilet was forever backed up and smelled like fresh turd. I hated using it. I turned off the water and ran back into my room. Josh was still in bed.

"Josh! Git your butt up!" I gave the bed another couple bounces and Josh rolled right out and hit the floor.

"Umph!"

By the time Josh and I walked into the kitchen, only two sausages were left on the table: one on each of our plates surrounded by some scrambled eggs. Momma was still at the stove stirring a pot filled with yellow, buttery grits. A plate on the counter next to the stove had a pile of eggs and sausages; I knew that was Momma's.

"Who's this?" Uncle Travis said, looking at Josh as we sat down at the table.

I didn't waste a second. I went right at the food like a starvin' dog.

"Slow it down, No Good!" Momma yelled.

Pa nodded his head at Josh. "Josh here is stayin' with us while Pastor Jim finds homes for all them kids he places."

"Orphan?" Uncle Travis asked.

"Josh ain't an orphan long as he livin' with us," Momma corrected. "He family. Besides, No Good's been happy as a hog to have a brother. They been side by side since he come. Ain't cha, No Good?"

My mouth full, I eyed Josh, and he eyed me back. If Momma had said what she said the day before, I might have agreed. I might have said that I liked having Josh here. But now, somethin' was different. Couldn't quite put my finger on it, but looking at Josh at the table felt like I was looking at Tommy J after he come struttin' in telling his tales all shirtless and nasty. It's not like they were alike. Josh wasn't nearly as homely or full of himself. Still, I felt about as comfortable being next to him.

"I said, ain't cha, No Good?"

I swallowed. "I don't know," I said truthfully. I scooped in another mouthful of eggs.

Momma turned away from her grits. "You don't know? You fergit what we talked about the day he come, did ya?"

My mouth full, I mumbled, "I 'membered."

Uncle Travis spoke up. "Cut the boy some slack, Em. No Good's been an only child his whole life. Now you stick 'im with a roommate and expect them to get along like kin? It ain't easy. I remember bunking with some unsavory boys during boot camp and I had to make do."

Momma shook her wooden spoon at Uncle Travis. "Josh here is a fine boy, Travis. And we talked about encouragin' No Good like that. He's gotta learn how to get along. Don't start fillin' his head with notions that hasslin' Josh is proper."

I looked at Josh. He was still nibblin' on his sausage and eyeing me. I looked away.

Uncle Travis smiled. "I wasn't tryin' to steer him wrong. I just know what it's like, that's all. I'm sure Josh is a fine boy. Just takes time."

"I'm sure they're all right," Pa said. "No Good's got a habit of shootin' off his mouth, but they gettin' along just fine."

Momma turned back to her grits and gave them a few spins with her spoon. "Yeah. They ain't killin' each other. But No Good still gotta learn how to get along."

"Besides," said Pa, "they the same age and all. They ain't that different. Ain't that different at all. Boys are boys after all."

Not sure what set it off, but I suddenly shot up from my seat. "Well," I yelled, "if you all know me so well, why'd you even ask?"

"Sit down, No Good," said Pa.

"I ain't sittin'! Everyone thinks they know what's goin' on in my head. You don't know me. And you don't know Josh. We a lot different. And it just so happen I don't want him here. I didn't ask for no brother. I was doin' fine and dandy without one. Ain't I enough for you?" I turned to Momma. "In fact, maybe God only wanted this family to have one boy. Why'd you think you got in that car wreck and messed up your insides, anyhow?"

"No Good!" Momma yelled, like a steam engine ready to blow. "Go...go to your room! Now!"

"Fine!"

I kicked the chair out, grabbed the Ted Williams baseball from the table, and started off toward the hallway. But I barely reached the entrance to the hall when Pa's giant hand grabbed my shoulder and spun me around.

"Boy, you apologize to your Momma, right now."

Pa scared me when he spoke business. But as soon as I looked at Josh, all the scared just slipped away and I said, "I ain't sorry."

It didn't take Pa but a second to grab my collar and drag me down the hall and throw me into my room. I stumbled and hit the floor. I rolled onto my back and propped myself up on my elbows. Pa stood at the door unfastening his belt, his face as red as a bull that hadn't pooped in the past week.

"Boy, you gotta learn to control that mouth." He spoke mad but steady like always.

Still, I couldn't stop. "How come I'm always wrong?"

"You can't be insulting your Momma like that." The last of his belt came snapping out like a whip.

"And you love her more than me?"

"It ain't about that. It's about respect."

"Nobody respects me. Nobody even wants me. Why else you call me No Good?"

He stopped and stood there breathing heavy and glaring me down. Seconds passed, my heart beating. Pa held his belt in his hands so tight, his knuckles were white. His face was solid and his brows low.

I opened my mouth to inhale, and he raised the belt up. I closed my eyes, held my breath, and clenched my teeth. He snapped it down.

WHAP!

I opened my eyes. The end of his belt was lying across the bed where he hit it. He hadn't hit me.

Sliding the belt away, he slowly threaded it back into his pants. I looked at his face as he said, "Boy...you've got to earn respect."

He turned and walked away.

I remained on the floor, still propped up on my elbows, listening to the squeaking of Pa's shoes down the hallway.

*   *   *

Several minutes later, I stepped out into the hall. I peered into the living room. Uncle Travis and Pa were jawing away, and Josh was sitting on a chair with his back to me. I stepped back and walked into the kitchen. Momma was alone at the table eating the last of her breakfast.

She looked up at me, her mouth full. "Well?"

"Sorry, Momma."

"You better be."

"Momma?"

"What?"

"There's somethin' you don't know about Josh."

She swallowed and waited.

Thirteen

The Half-Breed

"Lance," Momma spoke from the entrance to the living room. I stood next to her.

Pa turned away from Uncle Travis and looked up at Momma. "Ya?"

Uncle Travis and Josh turned to Momma. Momma glanced quickly at Josh and then turned away as she said, "We've gotta talk." She paused then added, "In our bedroom."

Pa shared a grave look with Uncle Travis and then nodded as he stood. The two walked past me to their bedroom, leaving me there staring at Uncle Travis and Josh.

"Uh-oh," Uncle Travis said in a low voice. Speaking to me he asked, "Now what'd you do?"

I shook my head and stepped into the living room. I sat down in Pa's squeaky rocker. It had Pa's familiar musk.

"Ooooh boy." Uncle Travis smiled at me. "When your momma and pa gotta talk about you in private, you must be in for a whopper."

"It ain't about me."

117

Uncle Travis shot a look at Josh still sitting there in the old lopsided wooden chair that Pa made when he was fifteen. Then he said to me, "Well, how you know that?"

I didn't say nothin'.

Uncle Travis looked at Josh again. Josh frowned and wiggled around in his chair like he had a chigger up his crawl.

A couple minutes later, Momma and Pa walked back in with their eyes set on Josh. The boy wiggled around a little more and swallowed good and hard.

Pa looked that boy up and down.

Momma stepped up to Pa and held his arm, still looking straight at Josh. "It don't matter, Lance," she said. "A boy's a boy. He needs a home no matter what."

"Yeah," Pa nodded. "You're right about that. He better off with us than anyone else."

Uncle Travis shot up from the sofa and put his hands on his hips. "Everybody gonna be talkin' in code? What's goin' on?"

Momma was about to speak, but Pa shushed her with the wave of his hand. "It don't concern you, Travis. This between us and the boys."

"Don't concern me?" He whipped his head back and forth. "I'm still part of this family, if I recall. Now, I wanna know what's goin' on. What's the boy done?"

"He didn't do nothin'."

"Then why you bein' all hush-hush? You keep lookin' at the boy like he some sort of half-breed."

"He is."

Everyone turned and looked at me as soon as the words came out. I'm not even sure why I said it. The words just came right out like they always do.

"No Good..." Momma said.

"He is?" Uncle Travis said.

And it's like I couldn't turn it off. I went right on talking. "His momma was a Negro."

"What? And you got this boy living with you?"

Pa shook his head slow and then stepped up to Josh and put his hand on his shoulder. "It don't matter, Travis. He family now."

"He ain't no family. I know you two been achin' to have yourself more babies ever since the accident, but you don't gotta bring no half-breed into the family. We got enough trouble as it is."

"Now, Travis. Settle down."

"I ain't settlin' down. Boy, you don't know what this kinda thing does to people. Makes 'em all crazy-like. And I seen it. There's this boy in our company who got a bit too friendly with one of them Japs and they had themselves a baby. Man…you'd think he crucified Jesus the way everyone treated that boy just for having the kid. Ain't no way you bringin' this into our family." Uncle Travis yanked Josh right out of his seat. "Git up!"

"Travis!" Ma yelled.

Josh stumbled forward. I stood up and caught him before he fell. Josh took one glance at me, shrugged, and shot me a dirty look.

Uncle Travis took a step toward Josh but Pa moved between them. "Travis, you settle yourself down. Ain't no use taking it out on the boy."

"Lance, you don't know what you gettin' yourself into. I'm doing this for your own good. That boy need to be shipped off to Eatonville with his own kind. Now, move!" Uncle Travis gave Pa a good shove. Pa fell backwards over our coffee table and hit the ground.

"Lance!" Ma shouted.

Uncle Travis grabbed Josh by the collar. Josh stumbled forward. Steadying himself, Josh grabbed Uncle Travis's giant hand and bit right into him.

"Ah!" Uncle Travis yelled. He yanked his hand away and examined it closely. "That little turd bit me!" He glared at Josh. "Lemme at 'im!"

Uncle Travis dove at Josh, but instead knocked into me. I fell back and hit my head on something, and everything went black. Ma screamed. Glass broke. I opened my eyes. The blurriness cleared, and I could see Pa and Uncle Travis going at it, knocking over furniture and wrestling back and forth. Pa threw a punch. Uncle Travis swung back. Their fists hit each other in watermelon smashing thuds. I was as scared as a fly in a web. I sucked in a breath so tight it felt like my lungs would never work again.

Then I saw somethin' I ain't never thought I'd see in a million years. Pa grabbed Uncle Travis, the man I thought was the strongest person I ever knew, and he threw him straight through the front door like a sack of trash.

Pa stepped through the open door and stood. I got to my feet and stumbled up behind him. The upper door hinge was ripped out of the frame and the door hung crooked. The screen door on the other side had fallen flat on the ground. I peered past Pa and saw Uncle Travis lying on the ground at the bottom of the steps to our porch.

"Holy mackerel," I muttered, realizing that Uncle Travis not only flew through the door, but also fell across the porch and down the steps.

Pa spoke up. I could tell he was mad, but he talked with an odd calmness like he did when he read me the riot act. "You get on out of here, Travis, and calm yourself down. Once you in a more hospitable mood, we can talk."

Uncle Travis sat up and shook his fist at Pa. "You shouldn'ta done that, Lance! I ain't never comin' back here again! Far as I'm concerned you ain't family no more!"

Pa went right on talking like Uncle Travis hadn't said nothin'. "Just go for a walk downtown and we can talk later."

Uncle Travis got to his feet. "I ain't comin' back. I ain't never comin' back! You...you Negro lovers!" He paused. "I want my bag. Gimme my bag!"

"Just go for a walk," Pa went on.

Momma pushed her way around me and then Pa. It took me a minute to realize what she was carrying. Once she got to the porch, she threw Uncle Travis's duffle bag straight at her brother. "Here! And don't come back!"

"Don't worry! I won't!" Uncle Travis grabbed his bag and trudged off down the road.

"You shouldn'ta done that," Pa said to Momma in a low voice.

Momma stomped her foot. "Look what he done, Lance. Look what he done."

"It's all right, Emily." Pa wrapped his arms around her, patting her softly.

They held each other as I stood there watching from inside. I turned away and looked around. The living room was in shambles. Broken chairs, broken table, broken window, broken lamps, broken picture frames, broken door. I paused as it suddenly occurred to me: Josh. Where was Josh?

With the creak of the floor, I turned to see Pa and Momma walking back in. "Where's Josh?" Pa asked.

I threw my palms up.

Fourteen

The Scar

Pa had told Josh that he wanted him to anchor me to the ground. Yet after Pa shooed me out the door to go look for him again, I couldn't help but think how many times I'd had to chase that boy down. He kept shootin' off like he had rocket up his butt and I had a match.

I ran down the road with them sausage and eggs bouncin' around in my gut, and I tried to keep my mind on where Josh ran off to this time. I ran past Cully's house and thought maybe he'd hide in there, but that didn't make no sense. Or maybe he'd be heading out to see his grandpappy, but the jail was too far off to walk to and he didn't have no coins for the bus. Or maybe he was headin' back to First Baptist—but I knew Josh was smart enough not to trust Pastor Jim, who was no doubt a bigger Negro hater than Uncle Travis.

It didn't take me more thinking to lead me back down the Stink Bug Trail. Partway down the trail, I stopped and grabbed my side where a stitch was diggin' right in. I was tryin' to breathe normal when I saw somethin' light-colored hanging from a briar bush. I pushed past a couple palms and pulled off a ripped square of the shirt that Josh had borrowed from me. I turned it over and saw streaks of blood.

I looked up and held my breath so I could listen. I could hear snapping twigs in the distance. I took off running toward the sounds, jumping over logs and zigzagging past trees and puddles of muddy ground.

I jumped out between a pair of bushes and there he was, sitting on the ground in front of a rotting log and staring out over Lake Monroe, where we first spotted Old Man Badeau just days before. I could see he was still breathing hard, but he was just sitting there, his legs out in front of him and one arm wrapped around himself like he was cold. With his other hand, he was drawing a picture in the mud with a pinecone.

I was breathing good and heavy, but the woods and water were so quiet, it made me want to hush. I breathed through my nose and held my side.

"I trusted you," Josh said, still staring out over the water.

I wiped the sweat from my forehead and rubbed my side. "I know."

"You know?" He twisted partway around and looked at me. His eyes were all tearing up over his red cheeks. "Then why'd you tell 'em? I trusted you."

"I...I'm sorry."

He turned back toward the water, twirling around the pinecone in his hand. "Now everything's ruined. Just like Grandpappy said."

"But he's in jail." I knew right away I shouldn't have said that.

He shot up and spun around. "I know! I know he's in jail!" He stomped on the ground and a few blotches of mud flew up over his pants, or really, my pants that he was wearing. I remembered getting those pants a couple years ago when Grandma Jackie came into town and was disgusted at what

123

Momma was dressing me in. Now too small for me, they fit Josh's runty body like they was new again.

"Well," I said, "what do you want me to do about it?"

Josh stared at me so intense, with his fists tight at his sides and brow all crinkled—he looked like his head was ready to pop. Then he spun around and stared out at the lake again.

I opened my mouth to speak, but he beat me to it.

"Grandpappy told me that we all ridin' the same train. You can't change the rails, but can you help pull each other along." He paused, and I wondered if he was gonna go on. He spun around and took a step toward me. "You didn't ask to be my brother, but I didn't ask to be yours neither. But here we are. Stuck. At least we were. Now where am I supposed to go? I got no one."

I swallowed. For once since I'd known Josh, he did all the talking and I didn't have spit to say. I opened my mouth both nothing came.

A rumbling filled the sky. I looked up and a pair of single engine Navy planes flew overhead. I thought for a moment about the Navy pilot that beat up on Josh's Momma and I wondered if he was in one of them planes.

"You ain't talkin' cause you know I'm right."

I looked to the boy. "Josh...Uncle Travis is kicked out. Pa wants you home. Momma wants you home."

"And you? You want me home?"

I swallowed again. "I..."

"I didn't think so."

"You didn't let me finish."

He stepped over the hollow log toward me. "You don't have to finish. I know how you feel."

I grabbed him by his shoulders. "No, you don't. You don't know me."

He threw up his arms and wiggled free. "I thought I knew you. I thought you were my friend. Guess I was wrong."

124

I grabbed his shoulders again. "I am your friend. I'm the best friend you've got."

He threw his arms up again, but this time, he swung his arm around and the pinecone still in his hand came slicing through the underside of my left cheek. "Ah!" I stumbled back. I touched my face and inspected my hand. Blood. I looked at Josh and he was holding the pinecone up, waving it at me like a knife.

I was stunned. Not so much from the cut on my face, but because of what Josh did to me. My face was bleeding but the pain was elsewhere.

Josh finally gave up on me. "Ah, you ain't worth it." He tossed the pinecone aside and took off walking. He brushed by me, hittin' shoulders. I moved to follow him but he said, "Good-bye, No Good."

I stopped. I ain't realized before that point how ugly the name "No Good" sounded. And it hurt more than anything I could've heard coming from him.

I watched in silence as Josh kept right on walking.

$$* \qquad * \qquad *$$

It took me so long to get back home that it was a good hour later before I reached my porch. I walked up the steps and Momma ran up to the door that still hung like a loose tooth. Her eyes were expectant until she got a good look at me.

"What'd you do to your face?" She lifted my chin.

"It's okay." The blood was mostly dry by now.

She let out a "tsk" and ran back inside. When she came out, she had one of Pa's old shirts dripping wet. She wiped at the blood.

"Ah, Momma!" I backed off.

"No Good. You can't leave it there. It'll get infected. Here." She handed me the shirt. "I'll get the iodine."

125

She disappeared and came back with the smelly bottle. I looked up at her and the expression on her face deflated.

"You tried your best," she said.

I turned away for a moment and then back to her. "Pa?"

"When you didn't come back right away, he took off to First Baptist. Said he'd get Officer Carter to help drive around."

"That tub of lard can't—"

"No Good, watch your mouth."

"I know." I spun around and looked down our street. Old Man Jones was squeaking away on his porch, smoking his pipe, and Mrs. Johnston was shuffling down the dirt road carrying another load of someone else's laundry. A pair of squirrels raced up the tree in our yard, and I could hear the snap and rustling of the leaves after they disappeared up the trunk. Beside the tree sat Momma's old Victory Garden. During the war she kept it up, growing cucumbers and tomatoes that we ate when they bloomed during the summer. Now the bugs and weeds have taken over and it was nothing but a rectangle of ugly in our front yard.

Momma stepped up from behind and scratched my back like she used to do when I was younger and sick in bed. The scratch was always rough, but it was one of the best feelings in the world. It was one of the few times Momma got to touch me without hitting me or scraping off my skin with a dishrag. I never once told her, but I wished she'd do it all the time.

From behind, she grabbed the shirt from me, poured some iodine on it, and reached around to dab my cheek. It stung like a hot needle. I cringed.

"Don't you worry none," she told me. "We'll find him. He couldn't have run off that far."

But I knew he did, and I had a feeling he wasn't never coming back. That feeling hung on me like a rope wrapped around my neck. I wanted to cry, if only I could get a clean breath.

Fifteen

Josh

Two days passed. No Josh.

We were at the table eating dinner when Cully's pa came banging on the new front door. Pa left the table and headed down the hall. I looked at Momma and we both jumped up and followed.

Cully's pa, with his deep voice and forever frown, spoke to Pa in a whisper, which to Momma and me in the living room sounded like a grumbling bear waking from a nap. Pa twisted around and gave us a wordless "Stay here." He stepped outside and closed the door. Right before he did, I caught a glimpse of the single blue revolving light of a cop car outside in the semi-darkness.

Momma placed her hand on my shoulder. I touched her hand with mine.

The door swung open and Pa looked Momma and me up and down. "Git your shoes on, Emily. We headin' out."

"But…I'll have to put the food away." She spun around and headed toward the kitchen.

"No. Leave it. Git your shoes and let's go. No Good. C'mon."

I jumped to it and headed out the door.

Outside, there were two cars: a cop car and Cully's pa's car. The cop car had an officer standing outside with the doors open. A small crowd of neighbors were emerging from their houses. I ran down to the cars, hoping to see Josh in one of them. The cop car was empty and the other had Cully and Jeannie quiet in the backseat.

Up on the porch, Pa was pushing Momma along, with Cully's pa following the two. Pa approached me and said, "In ya go." Momma and I stuffed into the backseat of the empty cop car. Pa sat in the front passenger seat.

The cop got in, turned on his siren, and drove us off as the curious neighbors moved out of the way.

I wanted so badly to ask where we were going and if they'd found Josh, but I couldn't. I could barely stop my heart from bouncing out of my chest. I turned to Momma on occasion, but she wore a tense, quiet look.

$$*\qquad*\qquad*$$

The stars were out by the time we reached the hospital. Officer Carter was waiting at the entrance to open the door. For once, he didn't look ticked off to see me. Instead, he was all business, stern and quiet.

Officer Carter waved us to follow him. Cully, Jeannie, and their pa had climbed out of their car and were heading our way. We all walked down the hallways, and nurses and people watched us as if they knew why we were there.

Officer Carter stopped at one of the rooms and nodded.

Momma saw him first. "Oh, Josh!"

We flew inside, and after the adults' bodies cleared, I could see Josh lying in a hospital bed. He was all bruised and battered, blood and mud and even bits of grass and leaves all over him. His nose was swollen like a beet, and both arms had fresh scrapes up and down like he had taken a roll in a briar patch.

Momma went crazy. "How can they leave him like this? He needs to be cleaned up. Why ain't they cleaning him up? Gimme a towel." She grabbed the blanket from a nearby bed and went at Josh's face.

A nurse standing to the side stepped up and pulled at Momma. "Now, Ma'am. You leave him be. Don't touch him, Ma'am. Leave him be."

"He needs to be cleaned up! Why ain't you cleaning him up? What do they pay you for?"

"Ma'am, please."

Pa stepped up to Momma. "Emily, c'mon. Listen to the nurse."

"He's just a little boy! He needs to get tidied up! They can't leave him like this!" She struggled from the nurse.

"Ma'am, leave him be."

"Please, nurse." Pa touched the nurse's arm. "I'll handle her."

The nurse backed away, and Momma kept going at Josh's face.

"C'mon, Emily. C'mon."

"He's just a boy! They can't keep taking away my little boys! It ain't right! It ain't right!"

Cully's pa stepped in to help.

"C'mon, Emily." The two men pulled her off and backed her to the door.

"They keep taking my babies! They can't! They can't do that!"

Pa and Cully's pa took her out in the hall and their voices got echoey. The nurse followed them out.

I turned toward Cully and Jeannie.

Jeannie was covering most of her face with her hands. She said, "I gotta step out. I can't… I can't…" She ran toward the door.

Cully rolled his eyes and said, "Oh, diddly…" and followed her out the door.

I was left alone with Josh.

I kept staring at him. He didn't move. I stepped around him and stood next to him. The blanket Momma had been using was lying across his chest. I glanced at the door to make sure the nurse wasn't looking, then I picked up the blanket and started going at his face where Momma left off. The mud and blood was already drying, and rubbing his face just smeared it.

I stopped and stared at him. His eyelids were red and swollen like he'd been beaten somethin' fierce. After a minute, my tears fell on his face. It soaked into the mud so I gave it another go with the blanket.

Josh suddenly took a deep breath. I jumped back and dropped the blanket. He shivered so violently, the bed rattled.

"Josh?" I whispered. "Josh?" a little louder.

He opened his eyes. They were hollow and empty. He mumbled, "Madam…Madam."

"Josh, it's me. It's your…it's your brother."

He shuttered, eyes still vacant. "Johnny?" He reached out a hand.

"Yeah. It's Johnny." I grabbed his hand. He felt cold, very cold. I could feel the wet of the mud and blood.

"Johnny…" he said again, sadder this time. His eyes moved left and right but didn't focus on anything.

"I'm right here, Josh. I'm right here. I won't leave you. I've…I've always wanted a little brother. I wanted you."

"Johnny…" The name came out of him like he was deflating. The shaking quieted and then silenced altogether.

"I'm right here, Josh. I'm right here," I kept repeating.

His eyes closed and his hand let go.

130

But I kept holding his hand tight. "I'm right here, Josh. I'm right here." But soon, even my words fell to a whisper. I said one final "I'm right here, Josh. I'm right here"—but my voice made no sound.

I fell on him and wrapped my arms around his broken body.

Sixteen

The Promise

A couple weeks later, I wandered outside alone. I found an old rusting can of oil partially buried in a ditch. I dug it up and hit it up and down my street with a stick. In the middle of my game, I saw Ansel staring down at me from up in a tree. He smiled with them big white teeth of his, and I nodded back. He probably wanted a smile in return, but I couldn't manage it.

I headed off down the road and wound up shufflin' down the Stink Bug Trail until I came to the hollow log where I last spoke with Josh. I sat on the ground. Storm clouds were rolling in over Lake Monroe, and it was hot and humid, but I didn't mind it none. I closed my eyes and listened to the birds on the small jut of land across the lake from me. They were chirping and fussing about. The sound of them made me happy.

"That's my favorite spot," a deep voice rumbled from behind me.

I about jumped out of my skin. I sprung up and spun around. It was Old Man Badeau. He was all scabbed and looked thinner than I last saw him.

"When you get out?" I asked.

"Just yesterday. Took them police and lawyers two whole weeks to figure out that the man who dun off'd Josh…" He hesitated, as if the word Josh hurt his mouth. He continued, "They figured he did that Tommy J boy too. They got that man in shackles and shipped up to Palatka by now. Besides, I think them security guards were mighty tired of lookin' at my ugly mug." He snorted weakly and it led into a cough that took some time to settle down.

I watched him take out that same old handkerchief that Josh had stolen from him. He wiped his mouth dry and finished it off with a sneeze that sounded like a sick trumpet. He tucked the handkerchief back into his pants pocket. I realized then that he was still wearing Pa's tan slacks. They were much dirtier now and ripped at the bottom.

He looked down at me. "You still broken up 'bout Josh, ain't cha?"

I nodded.

"Yep," he said in a long drawl, like he was just as broken up. "Bet you is." He stepped his way around the hollow log with a limp and sat down on a stump. "It's hard losing someone, no matter what age you is. Even this old fool got it bad, yes sir." He leaned to the side, wiggled out that handkerchief again, and gave his face a wipe-down. "I remember when I was your age. Prob'ly had the best friends of my life then. Yep. And to lose a boy like Josh…" He barely got Josh's name out, like he had peanut butter stuck in his mouth.

"He…he told me you was his grandpappy," I blurted.

Old Man Badeau raised his eyebrows. "Ah, did he?"

"Yeah. Said you told him not to tell. But he did anyhow."

The old Negro nodded slowly and looked up at the sky. "It's gonna rain soon." A tear trickled down his face, and he fanned it off with his handkerchief.

"Is it true?"

He looked at me. "Yeah. 'Fraid so." He took a breath and looked me over. "You told your ma and pa, dincha?"

I looked down at my lap and nodded. "Yeah...and now...and now Josh dead, and it's all my—" My body shook with tears falling out like a rainstorm.

"Now, now..." Old Man Badeau placed his heavy hand on my shoulder. "There's some things you can control in life, but some things that jus happen to ya. Now that killer...Josh didn't ask him. Neither did Tommy J—and *he* wusn't your fault neither."

"Who was he? The killer?" I gave my face a swipe of my arm.

"Oh...jist some sick man. A real sick man."

"Why'd he dun it?"

Old Man Badeau wrinkled his brow and pulled at his chin. "There are some people who see somethin' they want and they take it, no matter the cost. Them the *real* devils in this world. And when they strike...they can turn your life upside down. All you got to do is make with what the Lord gives you."

I nodded, still unable to meet the old man's gaze.

"Besides," he went on, "Josh put you in a real pickle. He told you his secret. No boy should have to live with a secret like that. Neither him nor you. Live honest. That's the only way."

The rain fell good and quick.

The old man shook off the rain. "Better head on home before you catch your death."

I didn't move.

"Go on, boy."

"What about you?"

"Ah...I've been wet before. Besides, I'm an old man. I shoulda died off years ago. I'm just waitin' for my time. But you got years ahead of ya. You should run off home before your ma gets all worried over you."

I stood up and stepped away from the old man. I peered down the Stink Bug Trail and wiped the rain from my face. I felt the deep scar below my left cheek and thought about Josh. I turned back. "What's your name?"

"Huh? I can't hear you with all this rain."

I spoke louder. "What's your name?"

"How come you wanna know my name? What's it to ya? I'm just an old fool."

I stepped closer to him. "Everyone 'round here just calls you Old Man Badeau. My friend Cully thinks you bewitched. That's all hogwash. I know Josh called you Grandpappy, but I can't be callin' you that considerin' I already got one." I paused. "So, what's your name?"

He studied me for a long while and eventually a smile spread across his wrinkled, bruised face. "The name's Clarence." He nodded and I smiled back. "And what's your name?"

"It's No—"

"What's that?"

I smiled again and said, "My name's Johnny."

He held out his hand. "Well, how do you do, Johnny?"

I shook his hand. It felt cold and heavy. "I'll see you 'round, Clarence."

"Git on back home."

I ran back through the Stink Bug Trail, headed up around the corner to my street, down the now-muddy dirt road, and to my front porch. I was breathing heavy by the time I hopped up the porch steps. Momma stood there with her arms folded, all stern and serious.

"I guess you expecting me to clean them muddy clothes of yours? I just done your laundry, No Good."

"Momma..."

Seeing my expression, the look on her face changed. "It's all right. Jist don't track mud on my floors."

"Momma..."

"What's the matter?"

"Momma…" I started crying. "I…I don't wanna be called No Good no more." I wiped my face.

Momma looked at me steady for what felt like a long, long time. Finally, she rubbed the rain from my hair and said, "Okay, Johnny. Now head inside."

*   *   *

Momma kept her promise. She made everyone else keep it too. She raised her voice and slapped her wooden spoon to anyone who called me No Good.

Even thirty-five years later, when I had to lay her down in the ground next to Pa's grave, I closed my eyes, prayed, and I heard Momma's voice: "Okay, Johnny"—like she was remembering her promise. I realized then that she was up there, cookin' up some tasty pancakes for my brother that she always wanted. And Josh was there gobbling them up and smilin' at her like he done every time I called him my brother.

Ever since that day, that scar on my face gets me all choked up. Then I feel the warm, rough press of Momma's hand on my back, and I know that they're nearby, saving me a plate.

Dear Reader,

Thank you for reading No Good. I find it exciting to share my love of storytelling with you that will, I hope, make you feel, make you think.

If you've enjoyed the book, I have a favor to ask. User reviews on Amazon.com are fantastic resources for fellow readers to understand the general feel of a book. I'd be eternally grateful if you can take a few minutes to login Amazon and let others know your thoughts and feelings about this book. What better way to tell the whole world that you actually like a "No Good" book?

Here's the link:

http://www.amazon.com/No-Good-John-Hope/product-reviews/1499662718/ref=cm_cr_dp_see_all_btm

And if you didn't like this book, well... keep it to yourself.

Thanks!

John R Hope

P.S. – If you are an educator, you can download free chapter-by-chapter comprehension questions here:

http://www.johnhopewriting.com/teachers.html

Author Interview
John Hope

Question 1: What inspired you to write No Good?
No Good began with a different story called "Through Cody's Eyes". Cody was the first story with which I really connected emotionally. I stayed up all night writing the last 10,000 words and sometime around 4am, I literary had tears streaming down my face as I typed. Unfortunately, when others read Cody, no one else really liked it. I realized although I had written deep, emotional characters, the story and theme were too thin to attract readers. I wanted to try again. In parallel with this, I had a desire to write an historical fiction. I read an article – now I don't recall who wrote it – but it talked about Sanford, Florida just after WWII and how this town had an interesting mixture of educated military personal and blacks intermingling with poorer communities made up of children and grandchildren of formal slaves and pre-war migrant farmers. This clashing of communities and the need to mature seemed the perfect setting for a coming-of-age story like No Good.

Question 2: No Good has a lot of strong themes about racism. How do you feel about this sensitive subject?
Categorizing people based on trivial things like race is despicable and lazy. It's far easier to assume things about people rather taking the time to get to know them and learning who they are. Obviously, when you live with a group of people there are some things you take for granted and assume. But people are wonderful because of what they do and how they treat other people. And people horrible for the same reasons. It isn't until you get to know people that you can rightfully say who they are. Judging people based on race is wrong.

Question 3: Please explain Josh's fate. Why did you do that to him?
I've had a lot of people ask me that. In fact, some have been rather angry at me because of what happened in the story. I understand it hurts when things like that happen to a character you really like. But this is Johnny's story. And sometimes horrible things need to occur to your most beloved characters for them to be the people they grow

to be. This happens in real life all the time. We all have things that happen to us that we'd rather not think about and wish we could erase. But good or bad, without these tragedies we wouldn't be who we are today.

Question 4: Do you plan on writing a sequel to No Good?
No. In general, I'm not a big fan of writing sequels. I'd prefer to focus on one really good story and then end it. No Good in particular is crafted not to have a sequel. It centers on a very definitive point in Johnny's life, after which he is never the same again. Any sequel would feel very different than this book as the main character would be different. I would rather move to a new story with new characters and setting.

Question 5: Did you enjoy writing No Good?
Absolutely. I approach writing as an adventure and I'm always looking for new adventures. In No Good, I got to go back in time to very specific part of Sanford in the 1940s and I met Johnny and Momma and Pa and Cully and Josh and Tommy J and Officer Carter and Uncle Travis. It was a wonderful trip.

Question 6: Did any other book influence the writing of No Good?
Yes. In truth, all books that I've read has an influence to my writing. But specifically for No Good, I think the greatest influences were Timothy Egan's The Worst Hard Time and one of my personal favorites Wilson Rawls' Where the Red Fern Grows. Egan's book was so detailed with everything American farmers had to go through and had such a great poignant mood, after reading this I really wanted to write something centered on family financially struggling to make ends meet. And Rawls' book, wow. I absolutely loved how this book made me feel. Rawls does such an expert job exposing the heart of a boy, I absolutely wanted to write a story that did the same. No Good is my attempt of doing so.

Question 7: Do you have any final words for your readers?
As Johnny had to learn, I'd encourage everybody – young and old – to not accept the labels people place on you. From a young boy,

everyone called Johnny "No Good". That is, until he met Josh who inadvertently showed him how to look past these labels and see people, including himself, for whom they really are. Like Johnny, it's up to you to find and define your name. Force others to learn you.

ABOUT THE AUTHOR

John Hope is an award-winning short story, children's book, middle grade fiction and nonfiction history writer. His work appears in science fiction/fantasy anthologies and multiple collections of the best of the Florida Writers Association. Mr. Hope, a native Floridian, loves to travel with his devoted wife, Jaime, and two rambunctious kids. He enjoys running, reading, and writing, and has a weakness for good southern barbeque.

Read more at www.johnhopewriting.com

NO GOOD

ALSO AVAILABLE IN OTHER FORMATS

www.johnhopewriting.com

OTHER BOOKS BY JOHN HOPE

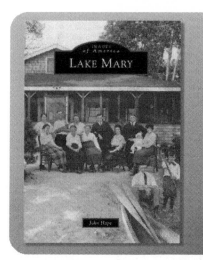

Images of America Lake Mary, Florida celebrates the town's history using over 200 archival photographs and presents the distinctive stories from the past that shape the character of the community today.

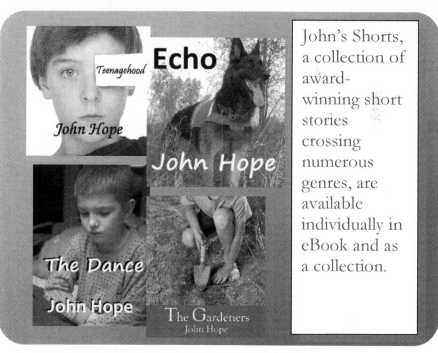

John's Shorts, a collection of award-winning short stories crossing numerous genres, are available individually in eBook and as a collection.

Made in the USA
Columbia, SC
03 October 2018